WORLD KITCHEN

MOROCCO

WORLD KITCHEN

MOROCCO

MURDOCH BOOKS

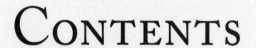

CONTENTS

MOROCCO'S FOOD PEDIGREE IS ENVIABLE
AND UNIQUE, WITH ARABIC, PERSIAN AND
ANDALUSIAN INFLUENCES, AS WELL AS
THE COOKING OF THE BERBERS.

Phoenicians and Carthaginians, Romans and Byzantines all had their time in what is now Morocco. The former traded along its Mediterranean shores in ancient times, planting olive trees and vines, while the empires of Rome and Byzantium included Mauretania, as it was then known, along with the remainder of North Africa. However, it was the forces of Islam erupting from Arabia in the late seventh century that had the most enduring influence on its culture, including its cuisine. To the Arabs, the area, from present-day Tunisia to Morocco, was known as the Maghreb (furthest west), a term still in use.

While Morocco's population is 80 per cent Berber, the people are regarded as Arab-Berber. There is also a significant population of Africans from Senegal, Mauritania and Mali. There are two official languages – Arabic and French, the latter from the French presence of 1912 to 1962. The French improved infrastructure and agriculture, planted vineyards and introduced viticulture. Their food legacy is baguettes, croissants, wine, coffee and some patisserie items.

The Berbers are believed to have originated in present-day Libya. Many of their customs continue today, such as their festivals and pilgrimages which last for several days. While the Berbers have their own language (with regional variations), it is not a written language. The culture of the Berbers today is strongly intertwined with Islam.

In 683, Arab soldiers reached Mauretania in their conquest to spread the message of the prophet, Mohammed, across North Africa. In 711, the Arabs, together with recruited Berbers, invaded the Iberian Peninsula (today's Spain and Portugal), dominating the region for the next seven centuries. As the Berbers were then known as Mauris, the invading forces became known as the Moors.

The Arabs named the peninsula Al Andaluz and introduced the cultivation of the saffron crocus, various citrus fruits, figs, pomegranates, spinach, eggplants, almonds, rice and sugar cane, and these subsequently filtered down to Morocco. The full extent of Arabic culture, learning, medicine, cookery, architecture and agriculture took flower in Al Andaluz, especially from the tenth century.

From the eleventh century to the thirteenth century, the Berber dynasties of the Almoravides and the Almohades ruled in Al Andaluz and Morocco. The lavish court kitchens of Fes, Rabat, Meknes and Marrakesh were the conduit by which new foods were introduced and recipes refined, a process that continued with later Berber dynasties. The cuisine that evolved makes the most of the ingredients Morocco produces in abundance, with flavours enhanced by new spices introduced by the Arabs. This is evident in dishes that use fruit for the sweet–sour flavours they impart, evolving into dishes that can only be Moroccan.

Traces of Ottoman cooking filtered into Morocco's north-east from Algeria, reached in the western expansion of the Ottomans. Stuffed vegetables can be attributed to this influence, as can the kebabs that are found all over Morocco. In some cafés, Turkish coffee is available, although it is usually French in style. Mint tea is the universal beverage.

The reconquest of Spain came to an end in Granada in 1492 with the expulsion of the Moors and Jews who would not convert to Catholicism. Many Jews settled in Morocco, with their recipes enriching the tapestry of Moroccan food.

With the discovery of the New World, tomatoes, potatoes, squash and sweet and hot capsicums (peppers) were adopted and added new dimensions to Moroccan cuisine. Dried hot, mild and sweet chillies and capsicums also gave them additional spices – chilli, cayenne pepper and paprika.

FROM THE PALACES

It was in the palaces of the ruling Berber dynasties of the fourteenth century that Moroccan cooking began to take shape. The lavish court kitchens were the conduit by which new foods and recipes were eventually introduced to household kitchens. The famed bestilla, a pie of pigeons redolent with herbs and spices, lemony eggs and sweetened almonds, enclosed in tissue-thin warkha pastry, eventually emerged – a marriage of Berber cooking and Arab influences drawn from its Persian heritage. Via the Silk Road, the Persians had learned the art of making thin pastry from the Chinese.

THE NORTH

Tetuan, Tangier and environs reflect Andalusian influences, making great use of olive oil, capsicums, tomatoes, saffron and wild artichokes, and include tortilla-like omelettes and rice dishes. There are even tapas bars in these cities – vestiges of Spanish Morocco (1912 to 1956). Tetuan is also famous for its nouga (nougat) – another Spanish influence. In Tangier, fish is plentiful, with Mediterranean and Atlantic fish caught in its waters. In the north-west of this region, the blossoms of the bigarade (Seville) oranges are distilled commercially to make zhaar (orange flower water).

In the Rif Mountains, the Berbers are fond of breks, a Tunisian favourite that has been adopted by Moroccans, and make couscous with sorghum, a grain with a buckwheat-like flavour. Azenbu is another popular couscous, made from green barley

toasted in a pan with wild thyme, then cracked and steamed, and served with a bowl of buttermilk. Chorba bissara, a soup of dried broad beans, is a local breakfast staple, and a market favourite. Walnuts and chestnuts thrive, both good market crops for local souks and north coastal cities.

From the northern city of Fes to the west coast at Rabat, the Sebou Valley and the Sais Plain is rich agricultural country – the bread-basket of Morocco. The area produces wheat, pulses, barley, sunflowers, olives, citrus fruits, grapes and vegetables, with rice grown in the Gharb region. Cattle is raised in this area but slaughtered at the yearling stage, with the beef not as full-flavoured as mature beef, and often referred to as veal.

CENTRAL MOROCCO
West of the Middle Atlas lies the city of Marrakesh, with its walls surrounded by date palms and orange groves. One of Marrakesh's famous dishes is tangia, a slow-cooked meat stew traditionally prepared by men. Another favourite is kneffa, a festive dish of fried warkha pastry layered with almond custard and toasted almonds. Tkout, which is better known as sellou, is a mixture of browned flour, almonds,

sesame and anise seeds, honey, cinnamon and butter, served in a peaked mound. Guests eat it communally with small coffee spoons.

In the eastern Middle Atlas at Kelaa el M'gouna in the Dades Valley lie the famous rose gardens, with the fragrant fresh roses used for rosewater, the dried buds for spice stores. In Ouarzazate, where buds are distilled to make rosewater, a Rose Festival is held in mid May. Saffron is grown in the region, with its centre at Taliouine in the Anti Atlas, west of Ouarzazate. On the eastern side of the Middle Atlas, bordering Algeria, are the Erfoud Oases – Tafilalt, Rissania, Seffalat, Aoufous and Jorf – with a million date palms comprising some 30 varieties of dates.

THE WEST COAST
The Chaouia region of fertile plains on the western coast, from Rabat to Casablanca, also produces a myriad of fruits and vegetables; fields of golden wheat and sweet corn, vineyards, olive and almond groves abound. The garden continues down along the southern Atlantic coast where maize, millet and barley are grown, ending with Agadir's orange groves. Argan trees grow inland between Essaouira

and Agadir and oil is extracted from the argan nut. Amalou is a delicious ground almond, argan oil and honey mixture, spread on bread for breakfast or for snacking.

Fish and seafoods proliferate along the coastline, benefiting from the bounty of the Atlantic Ocean. Popular seafood dishes are sardin mraqad (fried sardines stuffed with chermoula), tagine bil hout (a fish tagine), kseksou bil hout (fish couscous) and bestilla bil hout (fish pie). Safi is famous for tassegal – bluefish – with Moroccans travelling from near and far to enjoy it in its season.

THE SOUTH

The Anti-Atlas and pre-Sahara region is home to the Berbers and nomadic Tuaregs. The couscous of these peoples is likely to be made from cracked barley, maize or millet, or from semolina. Meat is likely to be camel, hedgehog or wild fox, but milk and buttermilk, dates, pulses and bread made from barley, millet or wheat are their staples. Azenbu is another popular couscous. Asida, a white maize porridge, is a staple; it is taken from the communal bowl with three fingers, and then dipped in melted smen before being popped into the mouth.

Asida, a white maize porridge, is a staple; it is taken from the communal bowl with three fingers, and then dipped in melted smen before being popped into the mouth.

EATING MOROCCAN FOOD

For any meal, there are rules to follow. Hands must be washed; in most households, washing hands in the bathroom is the norm, but at a formal gathering a young family member or servant circulates the table with a jug of warm water, a basin and a linen towel. The fingers of the right hand are rinsed over the basin and dried on the proffered towel.

The table, usually round, is positioned in a corner in front of two banquettes, with chairs placed where necessary. A wedge of bread is placed before each diner generally by a daughter of the household, with more bread passed around during the meal. Vegetable dishes and salads are served in shallow bowls at the beginning of the meal, and are then either removed before the main meal, or left on the table to be picked at. The main meal is served in a tagine or on a large platter, which is placed in the centre of the table within easy reach. Morsels of food are picked from the communal dish with the thumb and first two fingers of the right hand, with food taken from the section of the dish that is nearest the diner. Pieces of bread are used to pick up food, soak up sauces and wipe fingers, for fingers are never licked during the meal. Water is served during the meal, but increasingly, soda drinks are preferred.

If the main meal is couscous, morsels of meat and vegetable are deftly combined with the couscous and rolled into a ball, then popped into the mouth. Spoons are also provided for those who prefer them. Hands are washed again when the meal is completed, this time more thoroughly; at formal gatherings, the washing water may be perfumed with rosewater, or the fragrant water is sprinkled over the hands after drying, using a special flask (rashasha). Guests then move to the living room for mint tea and pastries

Chapter 1

STREET FOOD

Whether it's hot chickpeas served with cumin in paper cones, kebabs cooked over a charcoal brazier or broad bean soup ladled from an earthenware jar, the range of street food is enticing.

Merguez bel Felfla wa L'basla
Lamb Sausages with Capsicum and Onion

Merguez, the spicy lamb sausage of the Maghreb, is much smaller than those sold in Western stores – only about 8 cm (3 in) long – with two sausages served on one piece of bread; one Western-made merguez sausage is usually sufficient per serve.

8 merguez sausages
1 green capsicum (pepper)
1 red capsicum (pepper)
1 large brown onion

2 tablespoons olive oil
2 rounds of Moroccan bread (page 59)
  or pitta breads, to serve

Prick the sausages with a fork, then cook them on a preheated barbecue grill over low–medium heat, turning frequently, for 8–10 minutes, until cooked through. Alternatively, cook the sausages in a chargrill pan.

Meanwhile, cut the green and red capsicum into quarters, remove the seeds and white membrane and cut into strips about 1 cm (½ in) wide. Halve and thinly slice the onion. Heat the oil in a frying pan on the barbecue, add the capsicum strips and onion and cook over medium heat, stirring often, for 10 minutes, or until tender. If the onion begins to burn, reduce the heat to low or move the pan to a cooler section of the barbecue. Season with salt and freshly ground black pepper.

If serving with Moroccan bread, cut the rounds into quarters. Arrange the sausages and a generous amount of the capsicum and onion mixture in the bread, or roll up in pitta bread. Alternatively, serve the sausages on plates with the vegetables, and the bread on the side.

SERVES 4

Ensure that you frequently turn the merguez sausages to promote even cooking.

Harira

Lamb and Chickpea Soup

A popular street food served with dates, harira is the break-the-fast soup of Ramadan. The Ramadan harira includes lentils and vermicelli, and is thickened for instant satiety after a day-long fast; dates and sweet pastries are traditional accompaniments.

500 g (1 lb 2 oz) boneless lamb shoulder
2 tablespoons olive oil
2 small brown onions, chopped
2 large garlic cloves, crushed
1½ teaspoons ground cumin
2 teaspoons paprika
1 bay leaf

2 tablespoons tomato paste (concentrated purée)
1 litre (35 fl oz/4 cups) beef stock
3 x 300 g (11 oz) tins chickpeas
2 x 400 g (14 oz) tins chopped tomatoes
3 tablespoons finely chopped coriander (cilantro) leaves
3 tablespoons finely chopped flat-leaf (Italian) parsley
coriander (cilantro) leaves, extra, to serve

Trim the lamb of excess fat and sinew. Cut the lamb into small chunks.

Heat the oil in a large heavy-based saucepan or stockpot, add the onion and garlic and cook over low heat for 5 minutes, or until the onion is soft. Add the meat, increase the heat to medium and stir until the meat changes colour.

Add the cumin, paprika and bay leaf to the pan and cook until fragrant. Add the tomato paste

and cook for about 2 minutes, stirring constantly. Add the beef stock to the pan, stir well and bring to the boil.

Drain and rinse the chickpeas, then add them to the pan, along with the tomatoes and chopped coriander and parsley. Stir, then bring to the boil. Reduce the heat and simmer for 2 hours, or until the meat is tender. Stir occasionally. Season, to taste. Garnish with the extra coriander.

SERVES 4

Cook the onions and garlic over low heat until the onions are soft and lightly golden.

ELADESS HARRA

Spiced Lentils

Most broad-bean soup sellers also offer these spicy lentils, ladled into bowls. When cooking green (also called brown) lentils, it is tempting to drain them after the first stage of cooking as the liquid is muddy, but in doing so, precious B vitamins are lost.

375 g (13 oz/2 cups) green lentils
2 large ripe tomatoes
3 tablespoons olive oil
1 brown onion, finely chopped
2 garlic cloves, finely chopped
1 teaspoon ground cumin
½ teaspoon ground coriander seeds

½ teaspoon turmeric
½ teaspoon paprika
⅛ teaspoon cayenne pepper
1 red capsicum (pepper), chopped
2 teaspoons tomato paste (concentrated purée)
3 tablespoons chopped flat-leaf (Italian) parsley
3 tablespoons chopped fresh coriander (cilantro) leaves

Pick over the lentils and place in a bowl. Wash with 2–3 changes of cold water, then drain in a strainer. Tip into a large saucepan and add 1 litre (35 fl oz/4 cups) water. Bring to the boil, then reduce to a simmer and cook for 30 minutes, skimming the surface as required.

While the lentils are cooking, halve the tomatoes crossways and squeeze out the seeds. Using the shredder side of a grater, grate the tomato halves down to the skin, discarding the skin. Set aside.

Warm the olive oil in a frying pan over medium heat, add the onion and cook for 5–6 minutes, or until soft. Stir in the garlic and spices and cook, stirring occasionally for 2 minutes, or until fragrant. Add the capsicum, grated tomatoes, tomato paste, parsley, coriander and 250 ml (9 fl oz/1 cup) water. Combine well, then add to the skimmed lentils. Season, partly cover with lid, and cook over low–medium heat for a further 25–30 minutes, or until the lentils are tender. Serve hot in bowls.

SERVES 4–6

Skim the surface of the water with a slotted spoon while the lentils are simmering.

BOULFAF

Liver Kebabs

Liver is held in high regard, and is served as fresh as possible. Vendors insert pieces of lamb fat between the liver cubes, or wrap each kebab with lamb caul fat to keep the liver moist. The oily marinade serves the same purpose, but do not overcook.

500 g (1 lb 2 oz) lamb liver in one piece
1 teaspoon paprika
½ teaspoon ground cumin
¼ teaspoon cayenne pepper
2 tablespoons olive oil

1 round of Moroccan bread (page 59) or pitta breads,
  to serve
ground cumin, coarse salt and cayenne pepper, or
  60 g (2 oz/¼ cup) harissa (page 242), to serve

Soak eight bamboo skewers in water for 2 hours, or use metal skewers.

Pull off and discard the fine membrane covering the liver. Cut the liver into 2 cm (¾ in) cubes, removing any tubes from the liver as necessary. Put the liver in a bowl and sprinkle with the paprika, cumin, cayenne pepper and 1 teaspoon salt. Add the olive oil and toss well. Set aside for 5 minutes.

Thread five or six pieces of liver onto the skewers, leaving a little space between the pieces. Cook on a barbecue grill or in a chargrill pan, brushing with

any of the oil remaining in the bowl. Cook for about 1 minute each side – the liver should remain pink in the centre, otherwise it will toughen.

If using Moroccan bread for the liver kebabs, cut the bread into quarters and slit each piece in half almost to the crust. For each serve, slide the liver from two skewers into the bread pocket. If using pitta bread, do not split it; just slide the liver from the skewers onto the centre and fold up the sides. Offer small separate dishes of cumin, coarse salt and cayenne pepper to be added to taste. If you are using harissa, stir 3 tablespoons hot water into the harissa and serve as a sauce.

SERVES 4

Ma' Quoda
Fried Potato Cakes

Potato cakes are often found in the weekly souks in remote regions and are easy to assemble. Potatoes are usually boiled in their skins, but peeling, slicing, then drying out the potatoes over heat, works just as well and is much kinder on the fingers.

600 g (1 lb 5 oz) boiling potatoes
2 garlic cloves, unpeeled
1½ teaspoons ground cumin
½ teaspoon ground coriander
1 teaspoon paprika
⅛ teaspoon cayenne pepper
2 tablespoons finely chopped flat-leaf (Italian) parsley
2 tablespoons finely chopped coriander (cilantro) leaves
2 small eggs
oil, for frying

Peel the potatoes, cut into thick slices and place in a saucepan with water to cover. Add the garlic and bring to the boil. Boil for 15–20 minutes until tender, then drain and return to medium heat to dry the potatoes, shaking the pan occasionally until the excess moisture evaporates. Squeeze the pulp from the garlic cloves into the potatoes, then mash. Add the cumin, ground coriander, paprika and cayenne pepper. Mix lightly and leave to cool.

Add the parsley, coriander leaves and one egg to the mash and season to taste. Mix well without overworking the mash. Divide into eight portions.

Lightly moisten hands and shape each portion into a smooth cake 1.5 cm (½ in) thick and about 8 cm (3¼ in) in diameter. Place on a baking tray lined with baking paper. Beat the remaining egg in a shallow dish.

In a frying pan, add oil to a depth of 5 mm (¼ in), and place over medium–high heat. When hot, dip the potato cakes one at a time into the beaten egg to coat completely and fry for 2–3 minutes each side or until golden and heated through. Drain on paper towel and serve hot.

PICTURE ON PAGE 24

MAKES 8

Dry the potatoes by shaking the pan over medium heat, then mash them with the garlic cloves.

Fried Potato Cakes (recipe on page 23)

BRIOUAT B'KEFTA

Lamb and Filo Cigars

Briouats are traditionally made with warkha pastry and can be shaped into triangles or cigar shapes. For street food, they are always fried. The following recipe uses filo pastry as a substitute and involves baking. It's easier to cook and healthier.

1 tablespoon olive oil
1 small brown onion, finely chopped
350 g (12 oz) lean minced (ground) lamb
2 garlic cloves, crushed
2 teaspoons ground cumin
1/2 teaspoon ground ginger
1/2 teaspoon paprika
1/2 teaspoon ground cinnamon

pinch of saffron threads, soaked in a little warm water
1 teaspoon harissa (page 242), or to taste
2 tablespoons chopped coriander (cilantro) leaves
2 tablespoons chopped flat-leaf (Italian) parsley
1 egg
8–12 sheets filo pastry
90 g (3 oz) butter, melted
1 tablespoon sesame seeds

Heat the oil in a large frying pan, add the onion and cook over low heat for 5 minutes, or until the onion is soft. Increase the heat, add the lamb and garlic and cook for 5 minutes, breaking up any lumps with the back of a wooden spoon. Add the spices, harissa and the chopped coriander and parsley. Season to taste and cook for 1 minute, stirring to combine.

Transfer the lamb mixture to a sieve and drain to remove the fat. Put the mixture in a bowl and allow to cool slightly. Mix in the egg.

Count out eight sheets of filo pastry. Stack on a cutting surface with the long side in front of you. Measure and mark the pastry into three strips and cut through the stack with a sharp knife to give strips about 12.5 cm (5 in) wide and 30 cm (12 in) long. Use extra sheets if the pastry is less than 38 cm (15 in) long. Stack the pastry strips in the folds of a dry cloth.

Place a strip of filo on the work surface with the narrow end towards you and brush with the warm, melted butter. Top with another pastry strip. Place 1 tablespoon of the filling 1 cm (1/2 in) in from the base and sides of the strip. Fold the end of the filo over the filling, fold in the sides and roll to the end of the strip. Place on a greased baking tray, seam-side down. Repeat with the remaining ingredients. Brush the rolls with melted butter and sprinkle with sesame seeds.

Preheat the oven to 180°C (350°F/Gas 4). It is best to do this after the rolls are completed so that the kitchen remains cool during shaping. Bake the briouats for 15 minutes, or until lightly golden. Serve hot.

MAKES 12

CHORBA BISSARA
Broad Bean Soup

The serving of street food begins early in the morning and this dried broad bean soup is a breakfast staple – warming, filling and delicious. It is ladled into bowls from a large, bulbous earthenware jar set at an angle over a charcoal fire.

350 g (12 oz/2 cups) dried, skinned and split broad
  (fava) beans or whole dried broad (fava) beans
2 garlic cloves, peeled

1 teaspoon ground cumin
1 teaspoon paprika
extra virgin olive oil, ground cumin and paprika to serve

Put the broad beans in a large bowl, cover with three times their volume of cold water and soak in a cool place for 12 hours. Drain and rinse before cooking. (If using whole beans, soak for 48 hours in a cool place, changing the water three or four times, then drain and remove the skins.)

Place the beans in a large soup pot, preferably of stainless steel. Add 1.25 litres (44 fl oz/5 cups) water, the garlic and spices. Bring to the boil, then simmer on low heat, covered, for 45–60 minutes,

until the beans are mushy; check and add a little more water if the beans look dry. Do not add salt or stir the beans during cooking.

Cool slightly and then purée the soup in batches. Reheat the soup and season to taste. Ladle into bowls and drizzle a little olive oil on each serve. Finish with a light dusting of paprika. Have extra olive oil on the table, and cumin and paprika in little bowls, to be added to individual taste. Serve with bread.

SERVES 6

Soak dried broad beans and then skin them before cooking.
Ready-skinned beans are more convenient.

Homus

Hot Chickpeas

Chickpeas are a staple in all Moroccan kitchens, a means of extending the protein content of meat tagines and soups. As street food, they are served in paper cones with a sprinkling of cumin and eaten with your fingers, or in small bowls with a spoon.

220 g (8 oz/1 cup) dried chickpeas, or 2 x 420 g
  (15 oz) tins chickpeas
2 tablespoons olive oil
1 brown onion, finely chopped

1 small green capsicum (pepper), chopped
1 teaspoon ground cumin
2 tablespoons finely chopped coriander (cilantro) leaves

To cook dried chickpeas, first soak them overnight in three times their volume of cold water. Drain and place in a saucepan with fresh water to cover well and simmer gently for 1 hour, or until tender, adding salt to taste towards the end of cooking. Drain, reserving 250 ml (9 fl oz/1 cup) of the cooking liquid.

If using tinned chickpeas, drain them, reserving 250 ml (9 fl oz/1 cup) of the liquid.

Warm the olive oil in a saucepan over medium heat. Add the onion and cook until lightly golden, then add the capsicum, cumin and coriander leaves and cook for a few seconds. Add the chickpeas and their liquid, and freshly ground black pepper, to taste. Bring to a simmer, cover and simmer until heated through.

Adjust the seasoning and serve hot in small bowls with bread.

SERVES 4–6

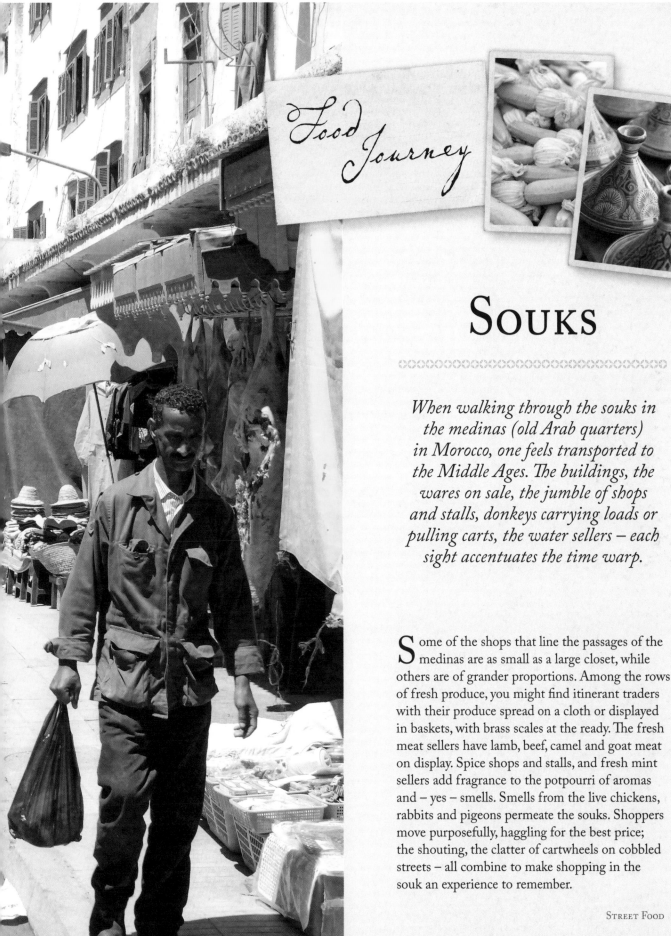

Food Journey

SOUKS

◇◇◇◇◇◇◇◇◇◇◇◇◇◇◇◇◇◇◇◇◇◇◇◇◇◇◇◇◇◇

When walking through the souks in the medinas (old Arab quarters) in Morocco, one feels transported to the Middle Ages. The buildings, the wares on sale, the jumble of shops and stalls, donkeys carrying loads or pulling carts, the water sellers – each sight accentuates the time warp.

S ome of the shops that line the passages of the medinas are as small as a large closet, while others are of grander proportions. Among the rows of fresh produce, you might find itinerant traders with their produce spread on a cloth or displayed in baskets, with brass scales at the ready. The fresh meat sellers have lamb, beef, camel and goat meat on display. Spice shops and stalls, and fresh mint sellers add fragrance to the potpourri of aromas and – yes – smells. Smells from the live chickens, rabbits and pigeons permeate the souks. Shoppers move purposefully, haggling for the best price; the shouting, the clatter of cartwheels on cobbled streets – all combine to make shopping in the souk an experience to remember.

Take time out for a glass of mint tea, hot and sweet, in which to dunk a hot doughnut; or take coffee at a café with a pastry just purchased from a nearby stall (you can do that in Morocco); or enjoy a glass of freshly juiced oranges heightened with the flavour of orange flower water. Perhaps visit a shop selling milk products, better known by its French name – laiterie (mahlaba) – for a bowl of milk pudding (mulhalabya), a portion of goat's cheese or a jar of yoghurt, sold plain and very sweet, which is the only way Moroccans eat it. Incidentally, a delicious yoghurt called raipe is made with the dried chokes of the little wild artichokes called coque, but this type of yoghurt has its season. In any souk you can tell by the produce being sold just what time of the year it is. Not all countries are as fortunate.

The water sellers are another one of the traditions of souk life, selling water to the thirsty. Wearing large-brimmed multicoloured hats festooned with bright tassels, their colourfully clad bodies gleam with brass-studded leather straps with clips for dangling chains, water cups, a bell and a leather water bag.

Fresh produce abounds in market stalls; everything from young zucchini with the blossoms attached to assure a special fragrance when cooked, to red onions freshly pulled from the earth. Crates of live chickens are ready for sale, with freshness certainly assured. Surrounding open-air stalls there could be shops selling ornate lanterns or household items, with spice shops perfuming the air. All show the diversity of traditional Moroccan souks.

QUOTBAN

Lamb Kebabs

Of all the street-food offerings, these would have to be the most popular. Little cubes of lamb fat are placed between the meat to keep the lamb moist as the kebabs cook over a charcoal fire. The oil in the following marinade serves the same purpose.

750 g (1 lb 10 oz) boneless lamb from leg
1 brown onion, grated
1 teaspoon paprika
1 teaspoon ground cumin
2 tablespoons finely chopped flat-leaf (Italian) parsley
3 tablespoons olive oil
1 round of Moroccan bread (page 59) or pitta breads, to serve

HARISSA AND TOMATO SAUCE
2 tomatoes
½ brown onion, grated
1 tablespoon olive oil
1 teaspoon harissa (page 242), or to taste, or ¼ teaspoon cayenne pepper
½ teaspoon caster (superfine) sugar

Soak eight bamboo skewers in water for 2 hours, or use metal skewers.

Do not trim the fat from the lamb. Cut the meat into 3 cm (1¼ in) cubes and put in a bowl. Add the onion, paprika, cumin, parsley, olive oil and a generous grind of black pepper. Toss well to coat the lamb with the marinade, then cover and leave in the refrigerator to marinate for at least 2 hours.

To make the harissa and tomato sauce, halve the tomatoes crossways and squeeze out the seeds. Coarsely grate the tomatoes into a bowl down to the skin, discarding the skin. In a saucepan, cook the grated onion in the oil for 2 minutes. Stir in the harissa or cayenne pepper, and add the grated tomatoes, sugar and ½ teaspoon salt. Simmer, covered, for 10 minutes, then remove the lid and simmer for 4 minutes, or until the sauce is thick and pulpy. Transfer to a bowl.

Thread the lamb cubes onto the skewers, leaving a little space between the meat cubes. Heat the barbecue grill to high and cook the kebabs for 5–6 minutes, turning and brushing them with the marinade. Alternatively, cook in a chargrill pan or under the grill (broiler).

If you are serving the kebabs with the Moroccan bread, cut the bread into quarters and slit each piece in half almost to the crust. Slide the meat from the skewers into the bread pocket and drizzle with a little of the tomato and harissa sauce. If you are using pitta bread, do not split it; slide the lamb from the skewers onto the centre, add the sauce and fold up the sides.

SERVES 4

QUOTBAN DEL KEFTA
Kefta Kebabs

These delicious sausage-shaped kebabs are deftly transferred into wedges of Moroccan bread by the vendors, often drizzled with a fiery harissa and tomato sauce (page 36). They are also made into small, round patties and chargrilled.

1 small brown onion, roughly chopped
2 tablespoons chopped flat-leaf (Italian) parsley
1 tablespoon chopped coriander (cilantro) leaves
500 g (1 lb 2 oz) minced (ground) lamb or beef
1 teaspoon ground cumin

1 teaspoon paprika
¼ teaspoon cayenne pepper
¼ teaspoon freshly ground black pepper
lemon wedges, to serve

Put the onion, parsley and coriander in the bowl of a food processor and process to a purée. Add the lamb, cumin, paprika, cayenne pepper, black pepper and 1 teaspoon salt. Process to a paste, scraping down the side of the bowl occasionally.

Divide the kefta mixture into eight even portions. Moisten your hands with water and mould each portion into a sausage shape about 9 cm (3½ in) long. Insert a flat metal skewer through the centre of each kefta sausage. Place on a tray, cover with plastic wrap and refrigerate for 1 hour.

Cook the kebabs on a hot barbecue grill or in a chargrill pan, turning frequently to brown evenly. The kefta are cooked until they are just well done (about 10 minutes) – they will feel firm when pressed lightly with tongs.

Serve the kefta kebabs with lemon wedges and salad greens. If desired, provide separate small dishes of ground cumin and salt, to be added according to individual taste.

SERVES 4

Right: Divide the kefta mixture into portions and mould into sausage shapes.

Far right: Insert a flat metal skewer into each kefta. Rounded skewers can cut through the kefta, causing them to fall off.

Chapter 2

HOME COOKING

The mix of textures and sweet and sour flavours that is indisputably Moroccan is embodied in recipes handed down through the generations, from mother to daughter, with each recipient adding their own touches.

Tagine Kefta 'Mchermel
Meatballs with Herbs and Lemon

The meatballs in this dish, tagine kefta 'mchermel, do not need to be browned. Spices, combined with fresh flat-leaf parsley and coriander, and the heat of fresh chilli, are used with lemon to make a delicious sauce in which to cook them.

½ brown onion, roughly chopped
2 tablespoons roughly chopped flat-leaf (Italian) parsley
2 slices white bread, crusts removed
1 egg
500 g (1 lb 2 oz) minced (ground) lamb or beef
½ teaspoon ground cumin
½ teaspoon paprika
½ teaspoon freshly ground black pepper

HERB AND LEMON SAUCE
1 tablespoon butter or oil
½ brown onion, finely chopped

½ teaspoon paprika
½ teaspoon ground turmeric
¼ teaspoon ground cumin
1 red chilli, seeded and sliced, or ¼ teaspoon
  cayenne pepper
375 ml (13 fl oz/1½ cups) chicken stock or water
2 tablespoons chopped coriander (cilantro) leaves
2 tablespoons chopped flat-leaf (Italian) parsley
2 tablespoons lemon juice
½ preserved lemon (page 247) (optional)

Put the onion and parsley in the food processor bowl and process until finely chopped. Tear the bread into pieces, add to the bowl with the egg and process briefly. Add the meat, cumin, paprika, black pepper and 1 teaspoon salt and process to a thick paste, scraping down the side of the bowl occasionally. Alternatively, grate the onion, chop the parsley, crumb the bread and add to the meat in a bowl with the egg, spices and seasoning. Knead until paste-like in consistency.

With moistened hands, shape the mixture into walnut-sized balls and place them on a tray. Cover and refrigerate until required.

To make the herb and lemon sauce, heat the butter or oil in a saucepan and add the onion. Cook over low heat for 8 minutes, or until softened. Add the

paprika, turmeric, cumin and chilli or cayenne pepper and cook, stirring, for 1 minute. Add the stock and coriander and bring to the boil.

Add the meatballs, shaking the pan so they settle into the sauce. Cover and simmer for 45 minutes. Add most of the chopped parsley and the lemon juice and season if necessary. Return to the simmer for 2 minutes. If using preserved lemon, rinse well under running water, remove and discard the pulp and membrane and cut the rind into strips. Add to the meatballs. Transfer to a tagine or bowl, then scatter with the remaining parsley and serve with crusty bread.

SERVES 4

Brek be Ton

Fried Tuna Pastries

To eat this Tunisian pastry (adopted by Moroccans), hold it by the corners, filling-side up, and bite into the egg, allowing the yolk to run into the tuna mixture. While spring-roll wrappers are used, warkha pastry is available in some Western markets.

2 tablespoons finely chopped brown onion
2 teaspoons olive oil
3 anchovy fillets, finely chopped
95 g (3 oz) tin tuna, in brine
2 teaspoons capers, rinsed, drained and chopped
2 tablespoons finely chopped flat-leaf (Italian) parsley

olive oil, for frying
4 x 21 cm (8¼ in) square spring-roll wrappers or
   warkha pastry rounds
1 egg white, lightly beaten
4 small eggs

In a small frying pan, gently cook the onion in the olive oil until softened. Add the anchovies and cook, stirring, until they have broken down. Tip into a bowl. Drain the tuna well and put it in the bowl, then add the capers and chopped parsley. Mix well, breaking up the chunks of tuna. Divide the mixture in the bowl into four portions.

Pour the oil into a large frying pan to a depth of 1 cm (½ in) and place over medium heat.

Put a spring-roll wrapper on the work surface and brush the edge with beaten egg white. Put a quarter of the filling on one corner of the wrapper, with the edge of the filling just touching the centre of the wrapper. Make an indent in the filling with the back of a spoon and break an egg into the centre of the filling. Fold the pastry over to form a triangle and firmly press the edges together to seal.

As soon as you have finished the first pastry triangle, carefully lift it up using a spatula to help support the filling, and slide it into the hot oil. Fry for about 30 seconds on each side, spooning hot oil on top at the beginning of frying. If you prefer a firmly cooked egg, cook for 50 seconds on each side. When the pastry is golden brown and crisp, remove with the spatula and drain on paper towel. Repeat with the remaining wrappers and filling. Do not be tempted to prepare all the pastry triangles before frying them, as the moist filling soaks through the wrapper.

Either eat the traditional way by holding the brek by the corners, or use a knife and fork.

SERVES 2

Reghaif

Filled Savoury Pancakes

These yeast-dough pancakes are flaky, light and crisp as a result of careful rolling and folding. The spiced kefta mixture is a substitute for a preserved spiced meat called khli' traditionally used in Morocco for these delicious snack breads.

2 teaspoons active dried yeast
1 teaspoon caster (superfine) sugar
350 g (12 oz/2¾ cups) plain (all-purpose) flour
oil, for shaping and frying

SPICED KEFTA
80 g (3 oz) smen (page 243) or ghee
250 g (9 oz) finely minced (ground) beef
2 tablespoons grated brown onion
4 garlic cloves, finely chopped
2 teaspoons ground cumin
2 teaspoons ground coriander

Dissolve the yeast in 125 ml (4 fl oz/½ cup) of lukewarm water and stir in the sugar. Sift the flour and ½ teaspoon salt into a bowl and make a well in the centre. Pour in the yeast mixture, then add another 125 ml (4 fl oz/½ cup) lukewarm water. Stir sufficient flour into the liquid to form a thin batter, cover the bowl with a cloth and leave for 15 minutes until bubbles form. Gradually stir in the remaining flour, then mix with your hands until a sticky dough is formed. If the dough is too stiff, add a little more water. Knead for 10 minutes in the bowl until smooth and elastic, then cover and leave in a warm place for 30 minutes.

To make the spiced kefta, heat the smen or ghee in a frying pan, add the beef and stir over high heat until browned. Reduce the heat to low, add the onion, garlic, cumin and coriander and season with salt and pepper. Cook, stirring, for 2 minutes, then add 500 ml (17 fl oz/2 cups) water. Cover and simmer for 30–45 minutes until the water

evaporates and the fat separates. Tip into a food processor and process to a paste; alternatively, pound to a paste in a mortar. Set aside to cool.

Using oiled hands, punch down the dough and divide into 12 balls. Oil the work surface and a rolling pin and roll out and stretch a dough ball into an 18 cm (7 in) circle. Spread thinly with a tablespoon of kefta paste. Fold the sides in so that they overlap, then fold in the top and bottom to overlap in the centre. Roll out and shape into a 9 x 13 cm (3½ x 5 in) rectangle. Place on an oiled tray and repeat with the remaining ingredients.

In a frying pan, add the oil to a depth of 1 cm (½ in). Place over high heat and, when almost smoking, reduce the heat to medium and add two pancakes. Cook for about 1 minute per side, or until browned and crisp and cooked through. Drain on paper towel and serve hot.

MAKES 12

TAGINE BEL HOMUS
Tagine of Chickpeas

An alternative to tinned chickpeas is dried chickpeas; for this recipe use 1 cup (220 g/8 oz), soaked overnight in cold water, drained and cooked with water to cover for 1–1½ hours. If preferred, do not skin the chickpeas.

3 tablespoons olive oil
1 brown onion, chopped
1 garlic clove, finely chopped
1 teaspoon harissa (page 242), or to taste,
   or ¼ teaspoon cayenne pepper
½ teaspoon paprika
¼ teaspoon ground ginger
½ teaspoon ground turmeric

1 teaspoon ground cumin
1 teaspoon ground cinnamon
400 g (14 oz) tin chopped tomatoes
1 teaspoon caster (superfine) sugar
2 x 420 g (15 oz) tins chickpeas
3 tablespoons chopped flat-leaf (Italian) parsley
2 tablespoons chopped coriander (cilantro) leaves

Put the olive oil and onion in a large saucepan and cook over medium heat for 7–8 minutes, or until softened. Stir in the garlic, the harissa or cayenne pepper, and the spices and cook gently for 2 minutes, or until fragrant. Add the tomatoes and sugar and season, to taste. Cover and simmer for 20 minutes.

Meanwhile, drain the chickpeas and put them in a large bowl with enough cold water to cover well. Lift up handfuls of the chickpeas and rub them between your hands to loosen the skins. Run more water into the bowl, stir well and let the skins float to the top, then skim them off. Repeat until all the skins have been removed.

Drain the chickpeas again and stir into the tomato mixture. Cover and simmer for 20–25 minutes, adding a little more water if necessary. Stir in the parsley and coriander and season, to taste. Serve with crusty bread or with couscous.

SERVES 4

Chickpeas are traditionally skinned for tagines so that flavours can be absorbed. Place soaked, cooked or tinned chickpeas in a bowl of water, rub handfuls together, and remove floating skins.

Marqa bel 'L'mloukhiya

Okra with Tomato Sauce

When preparing fresh okra, carefully trim the tip of each stem only, leaving most of the stem in place. If you cut into the okra itself, the viscous substance it contains becomes more noticeable. Always stir gently, or shake the pan, during cooking.

3 tablespoons olive oil
1 brown onion, chopped
2 garlic cloves, crushed
500 g (1 lb 2 oz) fresh okra, or 800 g (1 lb 12 oz)
   tinned okra, rinsed and drained

400 g (14 oz) tin chopped tomatoes
2 teaspoons caster (superfine) sugar
3 tablespoons lemon juice
3 large handfuls coriander (cilantro) leaves,
   finely chopped

Heat the oil in a large frying pan over medium heat, add the onion and cook for 5 minutes, or until the onion is softened. Add the garlic and cook for another minute. If using fresh okra, add it to the pan and cook, stirring occasionally, for 4–5 minutes.

Add the tomatoes, sugar and lemon juice and simmer, covered, for 3–4 minutes. Stir in the coriander (and the tinned okra, if using), cover and simmer for 5 minutes, then serve.

SERVES 4–6

Khizou Harra

Spiced Carrots

While this is served as an appetizer salad before a meal, it also makes an ideal vegetable accompaniment. The spices enhance the flavour of the carrots and the lemon juice counterbalances their sweetness.

500 g (1 lb 2 oz) carrots, cut into 6 x 1.5 cm
   (2½ x ½ in) sticks
½ teaspoon paprika
½ teaspoon ground cumin

2 tablespoons finely chopped flat-leaf (Italian) parsley
1 tablespoon lemon juice
2 tablespoons olive oil

Cook the carrot sticks in boiling, salted water for 10 minutes, or until tender. Drain and toss lightly with the paprika, cumin, parsley, lemon juice and olive oil and season with salt.

Place in a serving bowl, cover and leave aside for 2 hours for the flavours to develop. Serve warm or at room temperature.

SERVES 4

SHLADA DEL BARBA BIL KAMOON
Beetroot and Cumin Salad

This warm beetroot salad, with flavours heightened by ground cumin, is one you will make again and again. If serving as part of a Moroccan dinner, dice the beetroot rather than cutting into wedges, so that it can be easily picked up with the fingers.

6 beetroot (beets)
80 ml (3 fl oz/⅓ cup) olive oil
1 tablespoon red wine vinegar

½ teaspoon ground cumin
1 red onion
2 tablespoons chopped flat-leaf (Italian) parsley

Cut the stems from the beetroot bulbs, leaving 2 cm (¾ in) attached. Do not trim the roots. Wash well to remove all traces of soil, and boil in salted water for 1 hour, or until tender. Leave until cool enough to handle.

In a deep bowl, beat the olive oil with the vinegar, cumin and a good grinding of black pepper to make a dressing.

Wearing rubber gloves so that the beetroot juice doesn't stain your hands, peel the warm beetroot bulbs and trim the roots. Halve them and cut into slender wedges and place in the dressing. Halve the onion, slice into slender wedges and add to the beetroot. Add the parsley and toss well. Serve warm or at room temperature.

SERVES 4–6

Gloved hands are a must when handling hot beetroot.
Rub gently and the skins and stem remains slip off easily.

Chorba Djej bil Kseksou

Chicken Soup with Couscous

Use a whole chicken suitable for stewing and cut it into eighths, or use chicken pieces for convenience. When cooked, the chicken must be tender enough for the meat to be easily removed from the bones.

1.5 kg (3 lb 5 oz) chicken
2 tablespoons olive oil
2 brown onions, finely chopped
½ teaspoon ground cumin
½ teaspoon paprika
½ teaspoon harissa (page 242), or to taste,
    or ¼ teaspoon cayenne pepper
2 tomatoes

1 tablespoon tomato paste (concentrated purée)
1 teaspoon caster (superfine) sugar
1 cinnamon stick
100 g (4 oz/½ cup) couscous
2 tablespoons finely chopped flat-leaf (Italian) parsley
1 tablespoon finely chopped coriander (cilantro) leaves
2 teaspoons chopped fresh mint
lemon wedges, to serve

Rinse the chicken under cold running water and drain. Joint the chicken into eight pieces by first removing both legs and cutting through the joint of the drumstick and the thigh. Cut down each side of the backbone and lift it out. Turn the chicken over and cut through the breastbone. Cut each breast in half, leaving the wing attached to the top half. Remove and discard the skin.

Heat the oil in a large saucepan, add the chicken and cook over high heat for 2–3 minutes, stirring often. Reduce the heat to medium, add the onion and cook for 5 minutes, or until the onion has softened. Stir in the cumin, paprika and harissa or cayenne pepper. Add 1 litre (35 fl oz/4 cups) water and bring to the boil.

Halve the tomatoes crossways and squeeze out the seeds. Grate the tomatoes over a plate, down to the skin, discarding the skin. Add the tomato to the pan, along with the tomato paste, sugar, cinnamon stick, 1 teaspoon salt and some freshly ground black pepper. Bring to the boil, then reduce the heat to low. Cover and simmer for 1 hour, or until the chicken is very tender.

Transfer the chicken to a dish using a slotted spoon. When it is cool enough to handle, remove the bones and tear the chicken meat into strips. Return the chicken to the pan with an additional 500 ml (17 fl oz/2 cups) water and return to the boil. While the soup is boiling, gradually pour in the couscous, stirring constantly. Reduce the heat, then stir in the parsley, coriander and mint and simmer, uncovered, for 20 minutes. Adjust the seasoning and serve with the lemon wedges and crusty bread.

SERVES 4–6

Tagine Lahm bil Mloukhiya wal Matisha
Beef Tagine with Okra and Tomatoes

To prevent the okra from breaking up during cooking, cooks pass a needle and thread through the conical stems of the pods, tying the thread to form a 'necklace'. When the tagine has to be stirred or removed, this is lifted with the end of a wooden spoon.

1 kg (2 lb 4 oz) beef chuck steak
3 tablespoons olive oil
1 brown onion, finely chopped
3 garlic cloves, finely chopped
½ teaspoon ground cumin
½ teaspoon ground turmeric
400 g (14 oz) tin chopped, peeled tomatoes

½ teaspoon caster (superfine) sugar
1 cinnamon stick
2 tablespoons chopped flat-leaf (Italian) parsley
1 tablespoon chopped coriander (cilantro) leaves, plus extra leaves, to serve
500 g (1 lb 2 oz) small fresh okra

Trim the steak and cut into 2.5 cm (1 in) pieces. Heat half the olive oil in a large saucepan over medium heat and brown the beef in batches, adding a little more oil as needed. Set aside in a dish.

Reduce the heat to low, add the onion and the remaining olive oil to the pan and cook gently for 10 minutes, or until softened. Add the garlic, cumin and turmeric, cook for a few seconds, then add the tomatoes, sugar, cinnamon stick, 1 teaspoon salt and a good grinding of black pepper. Return all of the beef to the pan and add the parsley, coriander and 250 ml (9 fl oz/1 cup) water. Cover and simmer over low heat for 1½ hours, or until the meat is almost tender.

Meanwhile, trim the ends of the okra stems – do not cut into the pods. Rinse the okra in a colander under cold running water. If necessary, add a little more water to the saucepan so that the meat is almost covered, and place the okra on top. Lightly sprinkle with a little salt, cover and simmer for a further 30 minutes. Do not stir during this stage of cooking.

Scatter with the extra coriander leaves and serve with crusty bread.

SERVES 4–6

One wonders if it is the shape of the okra that appeals to Moroccans, or the taste. Certainly they make the most of its shape when presenting a cooked dish.

Shlada Litchine wa'L'fegel
Orange and Radish Salad

3 sweet oranges
12 red radishes
1 tablespoon lemon juice
2 teaspoons caster (superfine) sugar

2 tablespoons olive oil
1 tablespoon orange flower water
ground cinnamon, to serve
small mint leaves, to serve

Cut off the peel from the oranges using a sharp knife, removing all traces of pith and cutting through the outer membranes to expose the flesh. Holding the oranges over a small bowl to catch the juice, segment them by cutting between the membranes. Remove the seeds from the orange segments, then put the segments in the bowl. Squeeze the remains of the orange into the bowl.

Drain the orange segments, reserving the orange juice, and return the drained oranges to the bowl.

Wash the radishes and trim off the roots. Slice thinly using a mandolin (vegetable slicer). Add to the orange segments.

Put 2 tablespoons of the reserved orange juice in a small bowl, add the lemon juice, sugar, olive oil and a pinch of salt. Beat well and pour over the salad. Sprinkle with the orange flower water, toss lightly, then cover and refrigerate for 15 minutes. Transfer to a serving bowl, sprinkle the top lightly with cinnamon and scatter with the mint leaves.

SERVES 4

Shlada Fekkous wa Zitoun
Cucumber and Olive Salad

4 Lebanese (short) cucumbers
1 red onion
3 teaspoons caster (superfine) sugar
1 tablespoon red wine vinegar
3 tablespoons olive oil

1/2 teaspoon finely crumbled dried za'atar, or 1 teaspoon finely chopped lemon thyme
90 g (3 oz/1/2 cup) black olives
flat bread, to serve

Wash the cucumbers and dry with paper towel. Do not peel the cucumbers if the skins are tender. Coarsely grate the cucumbers, mix the grated flesh with 1/2 teaspoon salt and leave to drain well.

Halve the onion and chop it finely. Add to the cucumber, along with the sugar and toss together.

In a small bowl, beat the vinegar with the oil, then add the za'atar, and freshly ground black pepper, to taste. Whisk the ingredients together and pour over the grated cucumber. Cover and refrigerate for 15 minutes. Scatter with the olives and serve with flat bread.

SERVES 4

KESRA

Moroccan Bread

The first task in a Moroccan household, especially in rural areas, is making the daily bread. As it only has to rise once, it is quick to make. Country bread usually is made with wholemeal flour, but the following version gives lighter loaves.

3 teaspoons active dried yeast
500 g (1 lb 2 oz/3⅓ cups) strong flour or plain
  (all-purpose) flour, preferably unbleached
200 g (7 oz/1⅓ cups) wholemeal (whole-wheat) flour

125 ml (4 fl oz/½ cup) lukewarm milk
2 tablespoons yellow cornmeal
1 tablespoon whole aniseed, toasted sesame seeds,
  black sesame seeds or coarse salt for topping

Dissolve the yeast in 125 ml (4 fl oz/½ cup) of lukewarm water. Sift the flours and 1½ teaspoons salt into a mixing bowl and make a well in the centre. Pour the yeast mixture into the well, then add 250 ml (9 fl oz/1 cup) lukewarm water and the milk. Stir sufficient flour into the liquid to form a thin batter, cover the bowl with a cloth and set aside for 15 minutes until bubbles form.

Gradually stir in the remaining flour, then mix with your hands to form a soft dough, adding a little extra water if needed. Turn onto a lightly floured work surface and knead for 10 minutes, or until the dough is smooth and elastic and it springs back when an impression is made with a finger. Knead in extra plain flour if the dough remains sticky after a few minutes of kneading.

As the dough requires only one rising, divide into three even-sized pieces. Shape each piece into a ball and roll out on a lightly floured work surface to rounds 23 cm (9 in) in diameter or 26 cm (10½ in) for flatter breads.

Sprinkle cornmeal onto baking trays. Lift the rounds onto the trays, reshaping if necessary. Brush the tops lightly with water and, if desired, sprinkle with any one of the toppings, pressing it in lightly. Cover the loaves with clean cloths and leave to rise in a warm, draught-free place for 1 hour. The bread has risen sufficiently when a depression remains in the dough after it is pressed lightly with a fingertip.

While the loaves are rising, preheat the oven to 220°C (425°F/Gas 7). Just before baking, prick them with a fork. Put the breads in the hot oven and bake for 12–15 minutes, or until the bread is golden and sounds hollow when the base is tapped. Cool on a wire rack. Cut in wedges to serve. Use on the day of baking.

PICTURE ON PAGE 60

MAKES 3 LOAVES

Moroccan Bread (recipe on page 59)

Tagine'L'ghanmi be Jelbana
Lamb Tagine with Peas and Lemons

Preserved lemons add a wonderful flavour to this delicious dish of lamb, green peas, fresh herbs and ground spices. While shelled fresh green peas are preferred, frozen peas also give good results.

1 kg (2 lb 4 oz) boneless lamb shoulder or leg
2 tablespoons olive oil
1 brown onion, finely chopped
2 garlic cloves, finely chopped
1 teaspoon ground cumin
1/2 teaspoon ground ginger
1/2 teaspoon ground turmeric
3 tablespoons chopped coriander (cilantro) leaves

3 tablespoons chopped flat-leaf (Italian) parsley
1 teaspoon dried za'atar or 2 teaspoons chopped
  fresh lemon thyme
1 1/2 preserved lemons (page 247)
235 g (9 oz/1 1/2 cups) shelled fresh or
  frozen green peas
2 teaspoons chopped mint
1/2 teaspoon caster (superfine) sugar

Trim the lamb and cut into 3 cm (1 1/4 in) pieces. Heat the olive oil in a large saucepan over high heat and brown the lamb in batches, transferring to a dish when cooked. Add more oil if required.

Reduce the heat to low, add the onion and cook for 5 minutes, or until softened. Add the garlic, cumin, ginger and turmeric and cook for a few seconds. Add 375 ml (13 fl oz/1 1/2 cups) water and stir to lift the browned juices off the base of the pan. Return the lamb to the pan with a little salt and a good grinding of black pepper.

Add the coriander, parsley and za'atar, then cover and simmer over low heat for 1 1/2 hours, or until the lamb is tender.

Separate the preserved lemons into quarters and rinse well under cold running water, removing and discarding the pulp and membranes. Cut the rind into strips and add to the lamb, along with the peas, chopped mint and sugar. Return to a simmer, cover and simmer for 10 minutes, or until the peas are cooked. Serve hot.

SERVES 4–6

Preserved lemon is essential for this delicious dish. Cut rinsed rind into strips and add towards the end of cooking.

Baha

Steamed Lamb with Cumin

This is a dish of simple but delicious flavours. When served as part of a Moroccan meal, morsels of lamb are pulled from the bone with the fingers. However, lamb can be sliced and served with beetroot and cumin salad (page 53) and tiny boiled potatoes.

1.25 kg (2 lb 12 oz) lamb shoulder on the bone
1½ teaspoons ground cumin, plus extra to
 serve (optional)
1 teaspoon coarse salt, plus extra to serve (optional)
½ teaspoon freshly ground black pepper

pinch of ground saffron threads
6 garlic cloves, bruised
10–12 flat-leaf (Italian) parsley stalks
1 tablespoon olive oil

Trim the excess fat from the whole shoulder of lamb if necessary. Wipe the meat with damp paper towel and then cut small incisions into the meat on each side.

Combine the cumin, salt, black pepper and saffron and rub into the lamb, pushing it into the incisions. Cover and leave for 30 minutes for the flavours to penetrate. Place the lamb, fat side up, on a piece of muslin (cheesecloth), top with half the garlic cloves and tie the muslin over the top.

Using a large saucepan onto which a steamer will fit, or the base of a couscoussier, fill it three-quarters full with water. If using a saucepan and steamer, check that the base of the steamer is at least 3 cm (1¼ in) above the surface of the water.

Cover and bring to the boil. Line the base of the steamer with the parsley stalks and the remaining garlic. Place the lamb on top and put folded strips of foil around the rim of the steamer. Put the lid on firmly to contain the steam. Keeping the heat just high enough to maintain a boil, steam the lamb for 2–2½ hours. Do not lift the lid during the first 1½ hours of cooking. The lamb should easily pull away from the bone when cooked. Lift it out of the steamer and remove the muslin.

Heat the olive oil in a large frying pan and quickly brown the lamb on each side for a more attractive presentation. This dish is traditionally served as part of a Moroccan meal, with the lamb taken from the bone with the fingers, accompanied with little dishes of coarse salt and ground cumin for extra seasoning.

SERVES 4

Right: Rub the spice mixture into the lamb, pushing it into the incisions.

Far right: Wrap the lamb in muslin (cheesecloth) to keep in the flavourings.

Djej Mechoui

Spiced Grilled Chicken

The Moroccan spices and sugar-dipped, grilled lemon quarters add an exotic touch to barbecued chicken. Pumpkin and sweet potato stew (page 69) goes well as an accompaniment and can be cooked on the barbecue alongside the chicken.

2 x 750 g (1 lb 10 oz) chickens
pinch of saffron threads
1 teaspoon coarse salt
2 garlic cloves, chopped
1½ teaspoons paprika
¼ teaspoon cayenne pepper
2 teaspoons ground cumin

½ teaspoon freshly ground black pepper
1 tablespoon lemon juice
1 tablespoon olive oil
2 lemons
2 tablespoons icing (confectioners') sugar
watercress, picked over, to serve

To prepare the chickens, cut them on each side of the backbone using poultry shears or kitchen scissors. Rinse the chickens and dry with paper towels. Open out on a board, skin-side up, and press down with the heel of your hand on the top of each breast to break the breastbone and flatten it. Cut deep slashes diagonally in each breast and on the legs. Using two metal skewers for each chicken, push both of the skewers from the tip of the breast through to the underside of the legs, which should be spread outwards so that the thickness of the chicken is as even as possible.

Put the saffron threads in a mortar with the salt and pound with a pestle. Add the garlic and then pound to a paste. Work in the paprika, cayenne pepper, cumin, black pepper, lemon juice and oil. Rub the spice mix into the chickens, rubbing it into the slashes. Cover and refrigerate for at least 2 hours, or overnight. Bring the chickens to room temperature 1 hour before cooking.

Prepare a charcoal fire or preheat the barbecue and place the chickens on the grill, skin-side up. Cook over medium heat for 20 minutes, continually turning the chicken as it cooks and brushing with any remaining marinade. The chicken is cooked if the juices run clear when the thigh is pierced. Cooking time can be shortened on a barbecue if a roasting tin is inverted over the chickens to act as a mini oven – reduce the heat to low to prevent burning. Transfer the chickens to a platter, remove the skewers, cover with a foil tent and leave to rest for 5 minutes before cutting in half to serve.

Quarter the lemons and dip the cut surfaces in the sifted icing sugar. Place on the barbecue hotplate. Cook briefly on the cut surfaces until golden and caramelized. Serve the chickens with the lemon quarters and watercress.

SERVES 4

Matisha Maasla

Sweet Tomato Jam

This confit of tomatoes has a fantastic flavour. It is worth the effort of using fresh tomatoes, and preparing them in the Moroccan manner; however 2 x 400 g (14 oz) tins of roma (plum) tomatoes, undrained, may be used instead.

1.5 kg (3 lb 5 oz) ripe tomatoes
3 tablespoons olive oil
2 brown onions, coarsely grated
2 garlic cloves, crushed
1 teaspoon ground ginger
1 cinnamon stick

¼ teaspoon freshly ground black pepper
¼ teaspoon ground saffron threads (optional)
3 tablespoons tomato paste (concentrated purée)
2 tablespoons honey
1½ teaspoons ground cinnamon

Halve the tomatoes crossways, then squeeze out the seeds. Coarsely grate the tomatoes into a bowl down to the skin, discarding the skin. Set aside.

Heat the olive oil in a heavy-based saucepan over low heat and add the onion. Cook for 5 minutes, then stir in the garlic, ginger, cinnamon stick and pepper and cook for about 1 minute. Add the saffron, if using, the tomato paste and tomatoes and season with ½ teaspoon salt.

Simmer the tomato mixture over medium heat, uncovered, for 45–50 minutes, or until most of the liquid evaporates, stirring often when the sauce starts to thicken to prevent it catching on the base of the pan. When the oil begins to separate, stir in the honey and ground cinnamon and cook over low heat for 2 minutes. Adjust the seasoning with salt if necessary.

Serve with other salads in the traditional Moroccan way – eaten with bread at the beginning of a meal. In Morocco, this is also used as a basis for some tagines or as a stuffing for fish. Store in a clean, sealed jar in the refrigerator for up to 1 week.

MAKES 625 ML (22 FL OZ/2½ CUPS)

This Moroccan way of preparing peeled and seeded tomatoes is worthwhile adopting. Halve crossways, squeeze out the seeds, then grate down to the skin.

Marak Gar'a Hamra wa Batat Helwa
Pumpkin and Sweet Potato Stew

Select a pumpkin with firm flesh such as Queensland blue, kent, butternut pumpkin or other winter squash such as hubbard or Turk's cap, but avoid the jack-o'-lantern type as its flesh becomes mush when cooked.

60 g (2 oz) butter
1 large brown onion, finely chopped
2 garlic cloves, finely chopped
1 teaspoon ground ginger
1 teaspoon ground turmeric
1 cinnamon stick
pinch of cayenne pepper, or ½ teaspoon
   harissa (page 242), or to taste

500 ml (17 fl oz/2 cups) vegetable or chicken stock
⅛ teaspoon ground saffron threads
600 g (1 lb 5 oz) butternut pumpkin (squash) or other
   firm pumpkin (winter squash), peeled and cubed
500 g (1 lb 2 oz) orange sweet potato, peeled and cubed
60 g (2 oz/½ cup) raisins
1 tablespoon honey
coriander (cilantro) leaves, to serve

Melt the butter in a large saucepan over low heat. Add the onion and cook gently, stirring occasionally for 5 minutes, until softened. Add the garlic, ginger, turmeric, cinnamon stick and the cayenne pepper or harissa. Stir over low heat for 1–2 minutes, or until fragrant. Pour in the stock, add the saffron, then increase the heat to medium and bring to the boil.

Add the pumpkin, sweet potato, raisins and honey and then season with salt and freshly ground black pepper. Cover and simmer for a further 15 minutes, or until all the vegetables are tender. Remove the cinnamon stick, transfer the vegetables to a serving bowl and scatter with coriander leaves.

Stews such as this are traditionally served as a hot or warm vegetable course after the appetizer salads, but can be served as a vegetable accompaniment to the main meal. This goes well with chicken.

SERVES 4–6

Peeling hard pumpkin or winter squash can be hazardous if it is very firm. Use a heavy knife to cut pumpkin into large pieces. Place cut surface on a board and remove skin as shown.

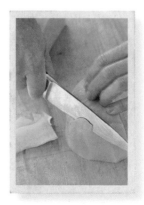

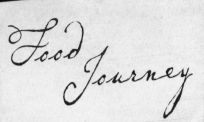

SPICE

◇◇◇◇◇◇◇◇◇◇◇◇◇◇◇◇◇◇◇◇◇◇◇◇◇◇◇

Arabs were involved in the spice trade for centuries before their foray across North Africa in the late seventh century. Via Moorish Spain, spices were introduced into Morocco, adding to those already used by the Berbers. The spicing skills of Moroccan cooks is the essence of their unique cuisine.

In the spice souks, the ground spices – reds, yellows and all shades of brown – are mounded high and smoothed in baskets, bins, bowls or bags. Whole spices – cassia bark and cinnamon quills, nutmeg, green cardamom pods and liquorice root, tears of mastic and gum arabic, dried chillies and fragrant dried rosebuds – contrast with smooth mounds of ground spices. The eight most important spices for Moroccan cooking are cinnamon, cumin, saffron (sold in small plastic containers to maintain freshness), paprika, turmeric, black pepper, felfla soudaniya (similar to cayenne pepper) and ginger (only dried ginger is used in cooking). Then there are cloves, allspice berries, bay leaves, fenugreek, aniseed, caraway, cumin and coriander seeds.

Tempting as the aromas might be, Moroccan cooks only purchase their spices in small amounts to ensure freshness, taking their purchases home in twisted paper packages to store in pottery jars.

Each spice shop has its own ras el hanout, which translates as 'top of the shop', or 'shopkeeper's choice'. This ground mixture may contain as many as 26 different spices and dried herbs, depending on the expertise of the shopkeeper. The mix may include black pepper, lavender, thyme, rosemary, ginger, nutmeg, cardamom, cinnamon, fenugreek, cloves and grains of paradise (melegueta pepper). Orris root, cubeb pepper, belladonna, rosebuds, hashish and other ingredients, some not available outside Morocco, might be included, depending, of course, on the shopkeeper.

Of all the spices, saffron reigns supreme, despite being the most expensive spice of all. Some shops offer more than just spices and dried herbs; they stock gnarled roots, berries and certain desiccated wildlife, ground and blended by the apothecary, according to a client's ailment. Much-loved orange flower and rosewater are also available. However, the amazing spectacle of perfect cones of spices, shaped each day with infinite care, epitomizes the importance of spices in Moroccan cuisine.

Tagine 'L'ghanmi bel Barkouk
Lamb Shank and Prune Tagine

The addition of prunes gives this dish a sweet–sour flavour, revealing its Persian origins. Any stewing cut of lamb may be used, but lamb shanks are delicious cooked in this way. Ask your butcher for frenched (trimmed) shanks for a neater appearance.

1 tablespoon oil
30 g (1 oz) butter
4 lamb shanks
1 brown onion, chopped
⅛ teaspoon ground saffron threads
½ teaspoon ground ginger

2 cinnamon sticks
4 coriander (cilantro) sprigs, tied in a bunch
zest of ½ lemon, removed in wide strips
300 g (11 oz/1⅓ cups) pitted prunes
2 tablespoons honey
1 tablespoon sesame seeds, toasted

Place a heavy-based saucepan over high heat and add the oil and butter. Add the lamb shanks and brown on all sides, then transfer to a plate.

Reduce the heat to medium, add the onion and cook gently for 5 minutes to soften. Add 375 ml (13 fl oz/1½ cups) of water, the saffron, ginger, cinnamon sticks and coriander sprigs and season, to taste. Stir well and return the lamb shanks to the pan. Cover and simmer over low heat for 1 hour, then add the lemon zest strips and cook for a further 30 minutes.

Add the prunes and honey, cover and simmer for a further 30 minutes, or until the lamb is very tender. Discard the coriander sprigs. Serve the tagine hot, sprinkled with sesame seeds.

NOTE: Frenched lamb shanks are trimmed of excess fat with the knuckle end of the bone sawn off. If unavailable, use whole shanks and ask the butcher to saw them in half for you.

SERVES 4

A small bunch of coriander sprigs adds flavour without altering the colour of the delicious prune sauce. Remove before serving.

Kseksou Bidawi
Couscous with Lamb and Seven Vegetables

The number seven is considered auspicious, hence the seven vegetables in this popular dish. The correct translation of 'bidawi' is 'in the style of Casablanca' (Dar-el-Beida in Arabic). In Moroccan households, couscous is served on Fridays.

1 kg (2 lb 4 oz) lamb shoulder, boned
3 tablespoons olive oil
2 brown onions, quartered
2 garlic cloves, finely chopped
1/2 teaspoon ground turmeric
1/2 teaspoon paprika
1/4 teaspoon ground saffron threads
1 cinnamon stick
4 coriander (cilantro) sprigs and 4 flat-leaf (Italian) parsley sprigs, tied in a bunch
400 g (14 oz) tin chopped tomatoes

1 1/2 teaspoons freshly ground black pepper
3 carrots, peeled and cut into thick sticks
3 small turnips, peeled and quartered
30 g (1 oz/1/4 cup) raisins
4 zucchini (courgettes), cut into sticks
400 g (14 oz) firm pumpkin (winter squash) or butternut pumpkin (squash), cut into 2.5 cm (1 in) chunks
420 g (15 oz) tin chickpeas, rinsed and drained
1 quantity couscous (page 244)
2–3 teaspoons harissa (page 242), to taste

Trim the lamb of excess fat if necessary, then cut into 2 cm (3/4 in) cubes.

Heat the oil in a large saucepan or the base of a large couscoussier and add the lamb, onion and garlic. Cook over medium heat, turning the lamb once, just until the lamb loses its red colour. Stir in the turmeric, paprika and saffron, add 750 ml (26 fl oz/3 cups) water, then add the cinnamon stick, the bunch of herbs, tomatoes, pepper and 1 1/2 teaspoons salt, or to taste. Bring to a gentle boil, then cover and simmer over low heat for 1 hour. Add the carrots and turnips and cook for 20 minutes.

Add the raisins, zucchini, pumpkin and drained chickpeas to the saucepan, adding a little water if needed to almost cover the ingredients. Cook for a further 20 minutes, or until the meat and vegetables are tender.

While the stew is cooking, prepare the couscous. Steam it either over the stew or over a saucepan of boiling water.

Pile the couscous in a deep, heated platter and make a dent in the centre. Remove the cinnamon stick and herbs from the stew and ladle the meat and vegetables into the hollow and on top of the couscous, letting some tumble down the sides. Moisten with a little broth from the stew. Pour 250 ml (9 fl oz/1 cup) of the remaining broth into a bowl and stir in the harissa. The harissa-flavoured broth is added to the couscous to keep it moist, and according to individual taste.

SERVES 6–8

BOUDENJAL MAQLI
Fried Eggplant Jam

Always select eggplants that are heavy for their size. This indicates that they are not over-ripe, with immature seeds for a better flavour. Salting does rid the eggplant of bitter juices, but can be omitted if you have chosen well.

2 x 400 g (14 oz) eggplants (aubergines),
　cut into 1 cm (½ in) thick slices
olive oil, for frying
2 garlic cloves, crushed
1 teaspoon paprika

1½ teaspoons ground cumin
2 tablespoons chopped coriander (cilantro) leaves
½ teaspoon caster (superfine) sugar
1 tablespoon lemon juice

Sprinkle the eggplant slices with salt and drain in a colander for 30 minutes. Rinse well, squeeze gently and pat dry. Heat 5 mm (¼ in) of the oil in a large frying pan over medium heat. Fry the eggplant in batches until golden brown on both sides. Drain on paper towel, then chop finely.

Put the eggplant in a colander and leave it until most of the oil has drained off, then transfer to a bowl and add the garlic, paprika, cumin, coriander and sugar.

Wipe out the pan, add the eggplant mixture and stir constantly over medium heat for 2 minutes. Transfer to a bowl, stir in the lemon juice and season with salt and pepper. Serve the eggplant jam at room temperature. Serve with bread as a dip, or with other salads.

SERVES 6–8

Cut the eggplant into thick slices before salting it to draw out any bitter juices.

SILQ BIL ROZZ

Silverbeet with Rice

Chard (silverbeet) is a popular vegetable throughout the Mediterranean region. It is a vegetable that children love to hate, and vegetable gardeners insist on planting because it grows so easily. The following recipe is an excellent way to prepare it.

900 g (2 lb) silverbeet (Swiss chard)
80 ml (3 fl oz/⅓ cup) olive oil
1 brown onion, chopped
1 teaspoon paprika

2 tablespoons chopped coriander (cilantro) leaves
2 tablespoons chopped flat-leaf (Italian) parsley
110 g (4 oz/½ cup) short-grain rice
1½ tablespoons lemon juice

Trim the ends of the stalks of the silverbeet. Wash well and cut the stalks from the leaves. Slice the stalks thickly and roughly shred the leaves.

Heat the oil in a large saucepan and add the onion. Cook over low heat for 5 minutes, or until soft.

Stir in the silverbeet stalks and paprika and cook for 5 minutes. Add the silverbeet leaves, coriander,

parsley, rice and 125 ml (4 fl oz/½ cup) water. Increase the heat to medium and stir until the silverbeet begins to wilt.

Reduce the heat to low, add the lemon juice and stir well. Simmer, covered, for 25 minutes, or until the rice is tender, stirring occasionally. Season, to taste, and serve hot as a vegetable accompaniment.

SERVES 4

This leafy member of the silverbeet family has been favoured in the Mediterranean region for centuries; combining it with rice and herbs reveals Andalusian influences.

Beyssara

Broad Bean Dip

To make this delicious dip, dried broad (fava) beans are soaked for 48 hours, and the leathery skin is removed. Fortunately Middle Eastern food markets now stock dried, skinned broad beans.

175 g (6 oz/1¼ cups) dried broad (fava) beans
   or ready-skinned dried broad beans
2 garlic cloves, crushed
½ teaspoon ground cumin
1½ tablespoons lemon juice

80 ml (3 fl oz/⅓ cup) olive oil
large pinch of paprika
2 tablespoons chopped flat-leaf (Italian) parsley
flat bread, to serve

Put the dried broad beans in a large bowl, cover with 750 ml (26 fl oz/3 cups) cold water and leave to soak in a cool place. If using dried beans with skins, soak them for 48 hours, changing the water once. If using ready-skinned dried beans, soak them for 12 hours only.

Drain the beans. If using beans with skins, remove the skins. To do this, slit the skin with the point of a knife and slip the bean out of its skin.

Put the broad beans in a large saucepan with water to cover and bring to the boil. Cover and simmer over low heat for 1 hour, or until tender (if the water boils over, uncover the pan a little). Remove

the lid and cook for a further 15 minutes, or until most of the liquid has evaporated, taking care that the beans do not catch on the base of the pan.

Purée the beans in a food processsor, then transfer to a bowl and stir in the garlic, cumin and lemon juice. Add salt, to taste. Gradually stir in enough of the olive oil to give a spreadable or thick dipping consistency, starting with half the olive oil. As the mixture cools it may become thicker, in which case you can stir through a little warm water to return the mixture to a softer consistency.

Spread the purée over a large dish and sprinkle with paprika and parsley. Serve with flat bread.

SERVES 6

Tagine 'L'ghanmi bel Btata wa Zitoun
Lamb Tagine with Olives and Potatoes

Saffron perfumes the potatoes and gives them a golden glow. If you can purchase cracked green olives, so much the better: blanch them for 2 minutes only each time, as the bitterness can be removed more readily.

1 kg (2 lb 4 oz) boneless lamb shoulder
3 tablespoons olive oil
2 brown onions, finely chopped
2 garlic cloves, finely chopped
1 teaspoon ground cumin
½ teaspoon ground ginger
½ teaspoon paprika

3 tablespoons chopped coriander (cilantro) leaves
3 tablespoons chopped flat-leaf (Italian) parsley
175 g (6 oz/1 cup) green olives
750 g (1 lb 10 oz) all-purpose potatoes
⅛ teaspoon ground saffron threads
1 tablespoon olive oil, extra

Trim the lamb and cut it into 3 cm (1¼ in) pieces. Heat half the oil in a large saucepan over high heat and brown the lamb in batches, transferring it to a dish when cooked. Add a little more oil as required.

Reduce the heat to low, add the remaining olive oil and cook the onion for 8 minutes, or until softened. Add the garlic, cumin and ginger and cook for a few seconds. Add 375 ml (13 fl oz/1½ cups) water and stir well to lift the browned juices off the base of the pan. Return the lamb to the pan, along with the paprika, ½ teaspoon salt and a good grinding of black pepper. Add the coriander and parsley, then cover and simmer over low heat for 1–1¼ hours.

Meanwhile, put the olives in a small saucepan and cover with water. Bring to the boil and cook for 5 minutes. Drain and repeat to sweeten the flavour. Add the drained olives to the lamb, cover and cook for 15–30 minutes, or until the lamb is tender.

Peel the potatoes and cut them into quarters. Put in a pan, cover with lightly salted water and add the saffron. Bring to the boil and cook for 10 minutes, or until tender. Drain the potatoes and toss lightly with the extra olive oil.

Transfer the lamb and sauce to a serving dish, arrange the potatoes around the lamb and serve.

SERVES 4–6

Tagine Lahm bil Batata Helwa
Beef Tagine with Sweet Potatoes

Use the orange-fleshed sweet potato as it is mealy and sweet, and keeps its shape when cooked. The tagine is finished and browned in the oven; in traditional Moroccan cooking, it would be covered with a metal lid with glowing charcoal placed on top.

1 kg (2 lb 4 oz) blade or chuck steak
3 tablespoons olive oil
1 brown onion, finely chopped
½ teaspoon cayenne pepper
½ teaspoon ground cumin
1 teaspoon ground turmeric

½ teaspoon ground ginger
2 teaspoons paprika
2 tablespoons chopped flat-leaf (Italian) parsley
2 tablespoons chopped coriander (cilantro) leaves
2 tomatoes
500 g (1 lb 2 oz) orange sweet potatoes

Trim the steak of any fat and cut into 2.5 cm (1 in) pieces. Heat half the oil in a saucepan and brown the beef in batches over high heat, adding a little more oil as needed. Set aside in a dish.

Reduce the heat to low, add the chopped onion and remaining oil to the pan and gently cook for 10 minutes, or until softened. Add the cayenne pepper, cumin, turmeric, ginger and paprika and cook for a few seconds, then add 1 teaspoon salt and a good grinding of black pepper. Return the beef to the pan, along with the parsley, coriander and 250 ml (9 fl oz/1 cup) of water. Cover and simmer over low heat for 1½ hours, or until the meat is almost tender.

Meanwhile, peel the tomatoes. To do this, score a cross in the base of each one using a knife. Put the tomatoes in a bowl of boiling water for 20 seconds, then plunge into a bowl of cold water to cool. Remove from the water and peel the skin away from the cross – the skin should slip off easily. Slice the tomatoes. Peel the sweet potatoes, cut them into 2 cm (¾ in) chunks and leave in cold water until required, as this will prevent them from discolouring. Preheat the oven to 180°C (350°F/Gas 4).

Transfer the meat and its sauce to an ovenproof serving dish (the base of a tagine would be ideal). Drain the sweet potatoes and spread on top of the beef. Top with the sliced tomatoes. Cover with foil (or the lid of the tagine) and bake for 40 minutes. Remove the foil, increase the oven temperature to 220°C (425°F/Gas 7) and raise the dish to the upper shelf. Cook until the tomatoes and sweet potatoes are flecked with brown and are tender. Serve from the dish.

SERVES 4–6

TAGINE 'L'GHANMI BE'MATISHA BAASLA
Lamb Tagine with Sweet Tomato Jam

Tomato jam is served as an appetizer, like a dip, but the same ingredients combine with lamb to give a beautifully flavoured tagine, redolent of cinnamon and honey. It is preferable to use fresh tomatoes rather than tinned.

1.5 kg (3 lb 5 oz) ripe tomatoes
1 kg (2 lb 4 oz) lamb shoulder or leg steaks
2 tablespoons olive oil
2 brown onions, coarsely grated
2 garlic cloves, finely chopped
1 teaspoon ground ginger
1/4 teaspoon freshly ground black pepper

1 cinnamon stick
1/8 teaspoon ground saffron threads
3 tablespoons tomato paste (concentrated purée)
2 tablespoons honey
1 1/2 teaspoons ground cinnamon
30 g (1 oz) butter
40 g (1 1/2 oz/1/4 cup) blanched almonds

Halve the tomatoes crossways. Squeeze out the seeds. Coarsely grate the tomatoes into a bowl down to the skin, discarding the skin. Set aside.

Trim the lamb steaks and cut into 3 cm (1 1/4 in) pieces. Heat half the olive oil in a heavy-based saucepan over high heat and brown the lamb on each side, in batches. Set aside on a plate.

Reduce the heat to low and add the remaining oil and the onion. Cook gently, stirring occasionally, for 10 minutes, or until softened. Stir in the garlic, ginger, black pepper and cinnamon stick and cook for 1 minute. Add the saffron and tomato paste and cook for a further 1 minute.

Return the lamb to the pan, along with the grated tomato, stir and season with salt and pepper. Cover and simmer gently for 1 1/4 hours. After this time,

set the lid slightly ajar so that the pan is partially covered and continue to simmer for 15 minutes, stirring occasionally. Remove the lid and simmer for a further 25 minutes, or until the sauce has thickened. When it is very thick, almost jam-like in consistency with the oil beginning to separate, stir in the honey and the ground cinnamon and simmer for 2 minutes.

Meanwhile, melt the butter in a small frying pan, add the almonds and cook over medium heat, stirring occasionally, until the almonds are golden. Tip immediately onto a plate to prevent them from burning.

Transfer the lamb to a serving dish, discarding the cinnamon stick. Sprinkle with the almonds. Serve with crusty bread or couscous.

SERVES 4–6

TAGINE OUMLIT BIL MATISHA
Tagine Omelette with Tomatoes

A typical dish made in the remote Middle Atlas, usually cooked in a tagine. Tomatoes are key to the flavour, and to duplicate this, one would have to peel, seed and chop a kilogram of vine-ripened tomatoes. Tinned roma tomatoes are just as good.

2 tablespoons olive oil
1 white onion, finely chopped
1 teaspoon ground coriander
1 teaspoon paprika
pinch of cayenne pepper

2 x 400 g (14 oz) tins roma (plum) tomatoes, chopped
3 tablespoons chopped flat-leaf (Italian) parsley
3 tablespoons chopped coriander (cilantro) leaves, plus extra coriander leaves, to serve
8 eggs

Use a 25–28 cm (10–11¼ in) non-stick frying pan with a domed lid to fit. Place the pan over low–medium heat and add the olive oil and chopped onion. Cook for 6 minutes, or until the onion is softened. Add the ground coriander, paprika and cayenne pepper and cook for a further 2 minutes. Add the tomatoes and their liquid, then add the chopped parsley and coriander. Increase the heat to medium, season and simmer for 10 minutes, or until the sauce is reduced and thick.

Break the eggs into a bowl and add 2 tablespoons of water. Season and beat lightly with a fork, just enough to combine the whites and yolks. Carefully pour the eggs over the back of a large spoon so that the mixture evenly covers the sauce. Cover with the domed lid and cook over medium heat for 15 minutes, or until the omelette is set and puffed. Scatter with the fresh coriander leaves and serve immediately. Serve with bread.

NOTE: To cook the omelette in a tagine, preheat the oven to 180°C (350°F/Gas 4). Make the sauce in a frying pan. Transfer the sauce to the tagine, cover and place in the oven for 10 minutes to heat the sauce. Remove the tagine from the oven and immediately pour the beaten eggs over the sauce. Cover and return to the oven for 5–8 minutes, or until the omelette is puffed and set. Serve at the table from the tagine.

PICTURE ON PAGE 90

SERVES 4

Right: Cook the tomato sauce until reduced and thick.

Far right: Pour the lightly beaten eggs over the back of a soup spoon to cover the sauce evenly.

Tagine Omelette with Tomatoes
(recipe on page 89)

Tagine 'Adess bil Gar'a Hamra
Spiced Lentils with Pumpkin

There are few truly vegetarian recipes in Moroccan cooking, but this is one of them, and a delicious and nutritious one at that. The earthy flavour of lentils combines with the sweetness of the pumpkin, the flavours melding with traditional herbs and spices.

275 g (10 oz/1½ cups) green lentils
2 tomatoes
600 g (1 lb 5 oz) firm pumpkin (winter squash) or butternut pumpkin (squash)
3 tablespoons olive oil
1 brown onion, finely chopped
3 garlic cloves, finely chopped
½ teaspoon ground cumin

½ teaspoon ground turmeric
¼ teaspoon cayenne pepper, or 1 teaspoon harissa (page 242), or to taste
1 teaspoon paprika
3 teaspoons tomato paste (concentrated purée)
½ teaspoon caster (superfine) sugar
1 tablespoon finely chopped flat-leaf (Italian) parsley
2 tablespoons chopped coriander (cilantro) leaves

Pick over the lentils and discard any damaged ones and any stones. Put the lentils in a sieve and rinse under cold running water. Tip into a saucepan and add 1 litre (35 fl oz/4 cups) of cold water. Bring to the boil, skim the surface if necessary, then cover and simmer over low heat for 20 minutes.

Meanwhile, halve the tomatoes crossways. Squeeze out the seeds and coarsely grate the tomatoes into a bowl down to the skin, discarding the skin. Set the grated tomato aside. Peel and seed the pumpkin and cut into 3 cm (1¼ in) dice. Set aside.

Heat the olive oil in a large saucepan over low heat, add the onion and cook until softened. Add the garlic, cook for a few seconds, then stir in the cumin, turmeric and cayenne pepper or harissa. Cook for 30 seconds, then add the paprika, grated tomato, tomato paste, sugar, half of the parsley and coriander, 1 teaspoon salt and freshly ground black pepper, to taste.

Add the lentils and pumpkin and stir well. Simmer, covered, for 20 minutes, or until the pumpkin and lentils are tender. Adjust the seasoning and transfer to a serving bowl. Sprinkle with the remaining parsley and coriander and serve hot or warm with crusty bread.

SERVES 4–6

Tangia

Slow-cooked Beef with Herbs

Tangia is a bachelor's dish, named for the earthenware amphora in which it is cooked. Ingredients are placed in the pot, the top sealed with parchment and string, then taken to the local bathhouse furnace room and cooked in the embers for hours.

1 kg (2 lb 4 oz) chuck steak or boneless beef shin
1½ brown onions, finely chopped
4 garlic cloves, finely chopped
2 tablespoons olive oil
2 teaspoons ras el hanout (page 242)
½ teaspoon harissa (page 242), or to taste, or
   ⅛ teaspoon cayenne pepper

¼ teaspoon freshly ground black pepper
3 ripe tomatoes
1½ preserved lemons (page 247)
2 teaspoons honey
1 tablespoon chopped coriander (cilantro) leaves
2 tablespoons chopped flat-leaf (Italian) parsley

Trim the beef and cut into 2.5 cm (1 in) pieces. Place the beef in a deep casserole dish. Add the onion, garlic, olive oil, ras el hanout, harissa and the black pepper and season with salt. Toss the meat with the marinade. Preheat the oven to 140°C (275°F/Gas 1).

Halve the tomatoes crossways. Squeeze out the seeds and coarsely grate the tomatoes down to the skins, grating them straight into the casserole. Discard the skins. Rinse the preserved lemons and remove the pulp and membranes. Chop the rind into chunks, reserving some for garnish, and add to the meat, along with the honey, coriander and 1 tablespoon of the parsley. Stir well, then cover and cook in the oven for 3½ hours. Juices from the meat should keep the dish moist, but check after 1½ hours of cooking and add a little water if necessary.

When the meat is very tender, transfer it to a serving dish, scatter over the reserved lemon rind and garnish with the remaining parsley.

SERVES 4–6

The preserved lemon should be rinsed before removing the pulp and membranes.

KHODRA BEL BARKOOK

Baked Vegetables with Prunes

While this would normally be cooked in a tagine over a charcoal fire, when baked, the vegetables and onions caramelize for extra flavour, further enhanced with ras el hanout. The prunes add a pleasant sweet–sour flavour to this dish.

60 ml (2 fl oz/¼ cup) olive oil
2 red onions, peeled and quartered
3 garlic cloves, unpeeled, bruised
2 sliced carrots
450 g (1 lb) pumpkin (winter squash)
450 g (1 lb) orange sweet potato

1½ teaspoons ras el hanout (page 242)
1 red chilli, seeded and sliced
375 ml (13 fl oz/1½ cups) light chicken or
    vegetable stock
200 g (7 oz/scant 1 cup) pitted prunes
1 tablespoon honey

Pour the olive oil into a 30 x 40 x 6 cm (12 x 16 x 2½ in) ovenproof dish and add the onions, garlic and carrots. Toss well. Bake in a preheated 200°C (400°F/Gas 6) oven for 15 minutes.

Peel and cut the pumpkin and orange sweet potato into large chunks. Add to the dish, along with the ras el hanout and red chilli. Season and toss well.

Bake for a further 30 minutes. Stir in the chicken or vegetable stock, prunes and honey and return to the oven for 30 minutes. Serve with steamed couscous or as a vegetable accompaniment.

SERVES 4

Far left: Cut firm, peeled pumpkin into large chunks.

Left: After the vegetables have partly baked, add the prunes, stock and honey and continue cooking.

DJEJ BIL MARAK SFARGEL
Chicken with Quince Sauce

Quinces are a popular addition to tagines. Following is a quick way to combine quince with chicken. While the recipe uses poached quince slices, you can substitute 90 g (3 oz) quince paste; mash it into the sauce and add a dash of rosewater.

1.5 kg (3 lb 5 oz) chicken, quartered
2 teaspoons ras el hanout (page 242)
2 tablespoons oil
1 brown onion, sliced

250 ml (9 fl oz/1 cup) chicken stock
4 slices quince in rosewater syrup (page 227)
1 tablespoon lemon juice
spiced carrots (page 49), to serve

Cut diagonal slashes in the breasts, legs and thighs of the chicken portions. Rub the ras el hanout into the chicken, cover and marinate for 20 minutes.

Heat the oil over medium heat in a large, lidded frying pan and add the chicken pieces skin-side down. Brown lightly for 2 minutes on each side. Add the onion around the chicken and cook for 5 minutes, or until the onion is soft. Add the stock and season if necessary with salt. Reduce the heat to low, cover and simmer for 45 minutes, turning the chicken occasionally.

Meanwhile, purée the quince with 2 tablespoons of their syrup. When the chicken is tender, add the quince purée and stir it into the pan juices. Add the lemon juice and stir well, then turn the chicken in the sauce. Simmer over low heat, uncovered, for 3–4 minutes, or until the sauce is thick. Serve the chicken with the quince sauce and spiced carrots.

SERVES 4

By slashing the chicken almost to the bone and rubbing in the ras el hanout, the spices penetrate the meat in the short cooking time of this delicious dish of chicken and quince.

Shlada Matisha wal Hamed Markad
Tomato and Preserved Lemon Salad

With its hot climate and fertile land, Morocco produces tomatoes that are richly red and luscious. This salad tempts the palate with its varied flavours. Serve it as an appetizer in the Moroccan manner, or as an accompaniment to chicken or lamb.

750 g (1 lb 10 oz) tomatoes
1 red onion
1 preserved lemon (page 247)
3 tablespoons olive oil

1 tablespoon lemon juice
½ teaspoon paprika
1 tablespoon finely chopped flat-leaf (Italian) parsley
2 tablespoons finely chopped coriander (cilantro) leaves

Peel the tomatoes by scoring a cross in the base of each one using a knife. Put the tomatoes in a bowl of boiling water for 20 seconds, then plunge them into a bowl of cold water to cool. Remove from the water and peel the skin away from the cross – it should slip off easily. Cut in half crossways and then squeeze out the seeds. Dice the tomatoes and put them in a bowl.

Halve the onion lengthways, cut out the root end, slice into slender wedges and add to the bowl.

Separate the preserved lemon into quarters, then remove the pulp and membrane and discard them.

Rinse the rind under cold running water, pat dry with paper towel and cut into strips. Add to the onion and tomato.

In a small bowl, beat the olive oil, lemon juice and paprika, and add ½ teaspoon salt and a good grinding of black pepper. Pour the dressing over the salad, toss lightly, then cover and set aside for 30 minutes. Just before serving, add the parsley and coriander and toss again. If preparing this salad ahead of time, cover the bowl and place in the refrigerator, but bring to room temperature before adding the chopped herbs.

SERVES 4

'L'khodra Maamera bel Kefta

Vegetables with Lamb Stuffing

Here is one version of Moroccan stuffed vegetables. Moroccan cooks take the time to hollow out the whole zucchini before filling them, but it is acceptable to halve them, scoop out the centres, fill them with the stuffing and re-assemble.

2 small capsicums (peppers)
4 zucchini (courgettes)
6 tomatoes

LAMB STUFFING
2 tablespoons olive oil
1 brown onion, finely chopped
2 garlic cloves, finely chopped
1/2 teaspoon ground ginger
1/2 teaspoon ground cinnamon
1/4 teaspoon freshly ground black pepper
500 g (1 lb 2 oz) minced (ground) lamb or beef
2 tablespoons chopped flat-leaf (Italian) parsley
1 tablespoon chopped coriander (cilantro) leaves

2 teaspoons chopped mint
55 g (2 oz/1/4 cup) short-grain rice

TOMATO SAUCE
1 tablespoon olive oil
1 brown onion, coarsely grated
1 garlic clove, finely chopped
1/2 teaspoon paprika
1/4 teaspoon ground cumin
1 large tomato, peeled, seeded and chopped
2 tablespoons tomato paste (concentrated purée)
1 teaspoon caster (superfine) sugar
1 tablespoon lemon juice

Cut the capsicums in half lengthways and remove the seeds and membranes. Cut the zucchini in half lengthways and scoop out the centres, leaving a 1 cm (1/2 in) border. Slice the tops from four of the tomatoes (reserve the tops), scoop out the centres and rub the pulp through a sieve into a bowl. Peel the skin from the remaining tomatoes (page 100), slice them thinly and set aside.

To make the lamb stuffing, put the olive oil and onion in a saucepan over medium heat and cook for 5 minutes. Stir in the garlic, ginger, cinnamon and pepper, then add the meat, stirring well to break up the lumps. Add 250 ml (9 fl oz/1 cup) water, the parsley, coriander, mint and 1 teaspoon salt. Bring to the boil, then cover and simmer over low heat for 20 minutes. Stir in the rice and cook, covered, for 10 minutes, or until most of the liquid has been absorbed.

To make the sauce, add all the sauce ingredients and 125 ml (4 fl oz/1/2 cup) water to the tomato pulp. Season. Preheat the oven to 180°C (350°F/Gas 4).

Loosely fill the vegetables with the stuffing: fill four zucchini halves and top each with an unfilled half, securing with wooden cocktail picks; fill the capsicums and arrange tomato slices over the top; fill the tomatoes and replace the tops. Arrange the vegetables in an ovenproof dish. Pour in the sauce, cover with foil and bake for 50 minutes. Remove the foil, baste with the sauce and cook for another 10 minutes, or until tender. Remove the cocktail picks from the zucchini and serve.

SERVES 4

CHAKCHOUKA

Tomato, Onion and Capsicum Salad

This salad is made every day in households for the midday meal. Moroccan peppers are not as fleshy as the popular capsicums; they are elongated and have a slight piquancy. If possible, use vine-ripened tomatoes.

2 green capsicums (peppers)
4 tomatoes
1 red onion
1 garlic clove, finely chopped

1 tablespoon finely chopped flat-leaf (Italian) parsley
80 ml (3 fl oz/⅓ cup) olive oil
1 tablespoon red wine vinegar

Cut the capsicums into large flattish pieces and remove the seeds and white membranes. Place the pieces, skin-side up, under a grill (broiler) and grill (broil) until the skin blackens. Turn them over and cook for 2–3 minutes on the fleshy side. Transfer the capsicum to a plastic bag, tuck the end of the bag underneath and leave to steam in the bag until cool enough to handle. Remove the blackened skin and cut the flesh into short strips. Place in a bowl.

Peel the tomatoes. To do this, score a cross on the base of each one using a knife. Put the tomatoes in a bowl of boiling water for 20 seconds, then plunge into a bowl of cold water to cool. Peel the skin away from the cross – it should slip off easily. Cut the tomatoes in half crossways and squeeze out the seeds. Dice the tomatoes and add to the capsicum. Halve the onion lengthways and remove the root. Cut into slender wedges. Add to the bowl, along with the garlic and parsley.

Beat the oil with the red wine vinegar and add ½ teaspoon salt and a good grinding of black pepper. Pour over the salad and toss well.

SERVES 4

K'DRA DJEJ

Chicken with Onions and Chickpeas

A k'dra is a berber method of cooking chicken, characterized by the large amount of herbed smen (clarified butter) and onions used, as well as chickpeas and saffron. The amount of smen has been reduced. Butter can be used instead of the smen.

60 g (2 oz) herbed smen (page 243) or butter
3 brown onions, thinly sliced
½ teaspoon ground ginger
½ teaspoon freshly ground black pepper
1.5 kg (3 lb 5 oz) chicken, quartered
⅛ teaspoon ground saffron threads

1 cinnamon stick
2 x 420 g (15 oz) tins chickpeas
3 tablespoons finely chopped flat-leaf (Italian) parsley, plus extra, to serve
lemon wedges, to serve

Melt the smen in a large frying pan. Add one third of the onion and cook over medium heat for 5 minutes, or until softened. Add the ginger, black pepper and chicken and cook without browning for 2–3 minutes, turning the chicken occasionally. Add the remaining onion, 310 ml (11 fl oz/1¼ cups) water, the saffron, cinnamon stick and 1 teaspoon salt. Bring to a slow boil, then reduce the heat to low, cover and simmer gently for 45 minutes.

Meanwhile, drain the chickpeas and place them in a large bowl with cold water to cover. Lift up handfuls of chickpeas and rub between your hands to loosen the skins, dropping them back into the bowl. Run more water into the bowl, stir well and let the skins float to the top, then skim them off. Repeat until all the skins have been removed. Add the chickpeas and parsley to the chicken and stir gently. Cover and simmer for 15 minutes, or until the chicken is tender.

Tilt the saucepan, spoon off some of the fat from the surface and transfer it to a frying pan. Lift out the chicken, allowing the sauce to drain back into the saucepan. Heat the fat in the frying pan and brown the chicken pieces quickly over high heat. Meanwhile, boil the sauce to reduce it a little.

Serve the chicken with the chickpeas and sauce spooned over. Sprinkle with the extra parsley and serve with lemon wedges and crusty bread.

PICTURE ON PAGE 106   SERVES 4

Chicken with Onions and Chickpeas (recipe on page 105)

Kefta Tagine bil Beid
Meatball Tagine with Tomato and Eggs

For communal eating in the Moroccan manner, this dish is served directly at the table in the dish in which it is cooked. With the aid of bread, diners manage to get their fair portion of the egg. Bread is also a must for mopping up the full-flavoured sauce.

700 g (1 lb 9 oz) minced (ground) lamb
1 small brown onion, finely chopped
2 garlic cloves, finely chopped
2 tablespoons finely chopped flat-leaf (Italian) parsley
2 tablespoons finely chopped coriander (cilantro) leaves
1/2 teaspoon cayenne pepper
1/2 teaspoon ground ginger
1 teaspoon ground cumin
1 teaspoon paprika
2 tablespoons olive oil
4 eggs

SAUCE
2 tablespoons olive oil
1 brown onion, finely chopped
2 garlic cloves, finely chopped
2 teaspoons ground cumin
1/2 teaspoon ground cinnamon
1 teaspoon paprika
2 x 400 g (14 oz) tins chopped tomatoes
2 teaspoons harissa (page 242), or to taste
4 tablespoons chopped coriander (cilantro) leaves

Put the lamb, onion, garlic, herbs and spices in a bowl and mix well. Season with salt and pepper. Roll tablespoons of the mixture into balls.

Heat the olive oil in a large frying pan over medium–high heat, add the meatballs in batches and cook for 8–10 minutes, or until browned all over, turning occasionally. Remove the meatballs and set them aside in a bowl. Wipe the pan with paper towel.

To make the sauce, heat the olive oil in the frying pan, add the onion and cook over medium heat for 5 minutes, or until soft. Add the garlic, cumin, cinnamon and paprika and cook for 1 minute, or until fragrant. Stir in the tomatoes and harissa and bring to the boil. Reduce the heat and simmer for 20 minutes.

Add the meatballs to the sauce, cover and simmer for 10 minutes, or until cooked through. Stir in the coriander leaves, then carefully break the eggs into the simmering tagine and cook until they are just set. Season, and serve with crusty bread to mop up the juices.

SERVES 4

Chapter 3

FESTIVE FOOD

Food served at banquets and religious festivals is spectacular, layered with Arab, Persian, Berber and Andalusian influences. It includes meltingly tender roast meat, tagines and couscous dishes sweetened with raisins.

Tagine Lham bel Teffah wa Zbib

Beef Tagine with Apples and Raisins

This is a robust beef tagine that is served when apples are in season, the tartness of the fruit mellowed with the addition of raisins, spices and honey. For a really authentic flavour, choose a thick, thyme-flavoured honey if possible.

2 tablespoons olive oil
40 g (1½ oz) butter
1 kg (2 lb 4 oz) beef chuck steak, trimmed and cut
   into 2.5 cm (1 in) cubes
1 brown onion, sliced
⅛ teaspoon ground saffron threads
½ teaspoon ground ginger

1 teaspoon ground cinnamon
4 coriander (cilantro) sprigs, tied in a bunch
125 g (5 oz/1 cup) raisins
3 tablespoons honey
3 tart apples, such as granny smiths
½ teaspoon ground cinnamon, extra
1 tablespoon sesame seeds, toasted

Place a heavy-based saucepan over high heat, add half the oil and half the butter and brown the beef in batches. Transfer to a dish when browned. Add the remaining oil as needed.

Reduce the heat to medium, add the onion and cook gently for 5 minutes, or until softened. Add the saffron, ginger and cinnamon and cook for 1 minute. Add 375 ml (13 fl oz/1½ cups) water, 1½ teaspoons salt and a generous grind of black pepper. Stir well and return the beef to the pan, along with the coriander sprigs. Cover and simmer over low heat for 1½ hours. Add the raisins and 1 tablespoon of the honey, then cover and simmer for 30 minutes, or until the meat is tender.

Meanwhile, halve the apples and remove the cores, then cut each half into thirds. Heat the remaining butter in a frying pan and add the apples. Cook, turning frequently, for 10 minutes. Drizzle with the remaining honey, dust with the extra cinnamon and cook for 5 minutes, or until glazed and softened.

Transfer the meat to a serving dish, pour the sauce over and arrange the apples on top. Serve hot, sprinkled with the toasted sesame seeds.

SERVES 6

Leave the skin on the apples and turn them frequently as they cook in the butter.

ZITOUN BIL HAMED

Warm Olives with Lemon and Herbs

While a choice of olives is given, a combination of both adds variety in colour and flavour. Boiling reduces salt content and 'sweetens' the olives. Cracked green olives can be difficult to obtain; if possible, use Sicilian green olives.

350 g (12 oz/2 cups) cured cracked green or black
   Kalamata olives
80 ml (3 fl oz/⅓ cup) olive oil
1 teaspoon fennel seeds
2 garlic cloves, finely chopped

pinch of cayenne pepper
finely shredded zest and juice of 1 lemon
1 tablespoon finely chopped coriander (cilantro) leaves
1 tablespoon finely chopped flat-leaf (Italian) parsley

Rinse the olives under cold water, then drain and place in a saucepan with enough water to cover.

Bring to the boil and cook the olives for 5 minutes, then drain in a sieve. Set aside. Add the olive oil and fennel seeds to the saucepan and heat gently until fragrant.

Add the garlic, olives, cayenne pepper and the lemon zest and juice. Toss for 2 minutes, or until the olives are hot.

Transfer the olives to a bowl and toss with the coriander and parsley. Serve hot with some crusty bread to soak up the juices.

SERVES 4

Shred the lemon zest finely; however, if you have preserved lemon on hand, use strips of rind instead.

Gar'a Shlada bil Hamed Markad
Warm Pumpkin Salad with Preserved Lemon

1 kg (2 lb 4 oz) firm pumpkin (winter squash)
   or butternut pumpkin (squash)
1 preserved lemon (page 247)
3 tablespoons olive oil
1 brown onion, grated
1/2 teaspoon ground ginger

1/2 teaspoon ground cumin
1 teaspoon paprika
2 tablespoons chopped flat-leaf (Italian) parsley
2 tablespoons chopped coriander (cilantro) leaves
1 tablespoon lemon juice

Peel the pumpkin, discard the seeds and cut into 2 cm (3/4 in) chunks. Set aside. Remove the pulp from the preserved lemon, rinse the rind, dice and set aside.

In a large, lidded frying pan, heat the olive oil over medium heat. Add the onion. Cook for 3 minutes, stir in the ginger, cumin and paprika and cook for a further 30 seconds. Add the pumpkin, parsley, coriander, lemon juice, the preserved lemon and 125 ml (4 fl oz/1/2 cup) water. Season to taste, then cover and simmer over low heat for 20 minutes, or until the pumpkin is tender, tossing occasionally with a spatula and adding a little more water if necessary. Serve the salad warm as an appetizer or hot as a vegetable accompaniment.

SERVES 4

Gar'a Hamra

Pumpkin Purée

A berber speciality of the Middle Atlas, this is made on the first day after Ramadan. The pumpkin is usually boiled, then fried, but as some pumpkins can become mushy very quickly, use the following method to prevent this.

750 g (1 lb 10 oz) firm pumpkin (winter squash) or
   butternut pumpkin (squash)
2 tablespoons oil
3/4 teaspoon ras el hanout (page 242)

1/2 teaspoon lemon zest, finely chopped
1 tablespoon lemon juice
1–2 tablespoons honey
2 teaspoons toasted sesame seeds

Preheat the oven to 200°C (400°F/Gas 6). Peel the pumpkin and discard the seeds, then cut into 2 cm (3/4 in) cubes. Put the pumpkin in a roasting tin with the oil and toss to coat.

Combine the lemon zest and lemon juice and pour over the pumpkin. Sprinkle with the ras el hanout,

then season and drizzle with the honey. Roast for 35 minutes, tossing occasionally with a spatula. Mash to a purée in the dish. Sprinkle with the sesame seeds and serve warm.

PICTURE ON PAGE 120

SERVES 4–6

Shlada bil Besbass wa Zitoun

Fennel and Olive Salad

2 fennel bulbs
125 g (5 oz/3/4 cup) black olives
2 tablespoons lemon juice

80 ml (3 fl oz/1/3 cup) extra virgin olive oil
2 tablespoons finely chopped flat-leaf (Italian) parsley
1 teaspoon finely chopped, seeded red chilli (optional)

Wash the fennel bulbs and remove the outer layers if they are wilted or damaged. Cut off the stems and slice thinly across the bulb to the base. Discard the base. Put the sliced fennel in a shallow bowl and scatter the black olives on top.

Beat the lemon juice with the olive oil in a jug. Season to taste and add the parsley. Add the chilli, if using. Beat well and pour over the fennel and olives just before serving. Toss lightly.

SERVES 4

Pumpkin Purée (recipe on page 119)

Tagine Djej bil Machmach
Chicken Tagine with Apricots

Whole chicken or chicken cut into portions is usual in Morocco. However, chicken breasts, off the bone and with the skin removed, are used in this dish to decrease the cooking time. When apricots are not in season, tinned apricots are a good alternative.

4 x 175 g (6 oz) skinless, boneless chicken breasts
40 g (1½ oz) butter
1 teaspoon ground cinnamon
1 teaspoon ground ginger
¼ teaspoon freshly ground black pepper
⅛ teaspoon cayenne pepper
1 brown onion, sliced
250 ml (9 fl oz/1 cup) chicken stock

6 coriander (cilantro) sprigs, tied in a bunch,
    plus extra to garnish
500 g (1 lb 2 oz) fresh apricots or 425 g (15 oz) tin
    apricot halves, in natural juice
2 tablespoons honey
1 quantity couscous (page 244)
2 tablespoons slivered almonds, toasted

Trim the chicken breasts of any fat. Melt the butter in a large frying pan over low heat. Add the spices and stir for 1 minute. Increase the heat to medium, add the chicken and turn in the butter. Cook for 1 minute on each side without allowing the spices to burn.

Add the onion to the pan around the chicken and cook for 5 minutes, stirring the onion and turning the chicken occasionally. Add the chicken stock and coriander sprigs and season if necessary. Reduce the heat to low, cover and simmer for 5 minutes, turning the chicken once.

Wash and halve the apricots and remove the stones. Place the apricots in the pan around the chicken, cut-side down, and drizzle with the honey. Cover and simmer for 7–8 minutes, turning the apricots after 5 minutes. Remove the chicken to a plate, cover and rest for 2–3 minutes. Slice each breast on the diagonal.

Put the hot couscous on serving plates and top with some sliced chicken. Remove the coriander sprigs from the sauce and spoon the sauce and apricots over the chicken. Scatter with the toasted almonds and the extra coriander and serve hot.

SERVES 4

Fresh apricots are turned only once in the sauce towards the end of cooking, to keep them intact.

Kseksou Tanjaoui
Couscous with Lamb and Raisins

This is one of the sweet couscous dishes served at diffas (banquets), the sweetness coming from the addition of raisins. The lamb shank meat cooks to melting tenderness, but other lamb cuts can be used, such as thickly cut shoulder chops.

60 g (2 oz) butter
3–5 lamb shanks, depending on size, untrimmed
2 brown onions, quartered
½ teaspoon ground turmeric
1½ teaspoons ground ginger
1 teaspoon freshly ground black pepper
⅛ teaspoon ground saffron threads

pinch of cayenne pepper
3 coriander (cilantro) sprigs and 3 flat-leaf (Italian)
  parsley sprigs, tied in a bunch
420 g (15 oz) tin chickpeas
1 brown onion, extra, halved and sliced
90 g (3 oz/¾ cup) raisins
1 quantity couscous (page 244)

Heat the butter in a large saucepan or the base of a large coussoussier. Add the lamb shanks, onion quarters, turmeric, ginger, black pepper, saffron and cayenne pepper and stir over low heat for 1 minute. Add 500 ml (17 fl oz/2 cups) water, the bunch of herbs and 1 teaspoon salt. Bring to a gentle boil, cover and simmer over low heat for 1¾–2 hours, or until the lamb is tender.

Meanwhile, drain the chickpeas and place them in a large bowl with cold water to cover. Lift up handfuls of chickpeas and rub between your hands to loosen the skins, dropping them back into the bowl. Run more water into the bowl, stir well and let the skins float to the top, then skim them off. Repeat until all the skins have been removed, then drain and set aside.

When the lamb is cooked, lift the shanks from the broth and strip off the meat. Discard the bones and cut the meat into pieces. Return the meat to the pan, along with the chickpeas, extra sliced onion and the raisins. Cover and cook for 20 minutes, adding a little more water to the pan if necessary.

Pile the hot couscous on a large, warm platter and make a dent in the centre. Discard the bunch of herbs from the lamb mixture, then ladle it into the hollow. Moisten with some of the broth and put the remaining broth in a bowl, which can be added as needed.

SERVES 6

Tagine 'L'ghanmi B'tamra
Lamb Tagine with Dates

In this rich and luscious dish, the dried dates are pitted, and are used to thicken the sauce, which carries their flavour through the dish. The whole dates used to complete the dish are left unpitted, otherwise they can disintegrate.

1 kg (2 lb 4 oz) boneless lamb from shoulder or leg
30 g (1 oz) butter
1 brown onion, finely chopped
1 teaspoon ground ginger
1 teaspoon ground cinnamon
½ teaspoon freshly ground black pepper
55 g (2 oz/⅓ cup) pitted, chopped dried dates

pinch of ground saffron threads
2 tablespoons honey
2 tablespoons lemon juice
200 g (7 oz/1¼ cups) fresh or dessert dates (unpitted)
½ preserved lemon (page 247)
15 g (½ oz) butter, extra
40 g (1½ oz/⅓ cup) slivered almonds

Trim the lamb and cut into 2.5 cm (1 in) cubes. In a large heavy-based saucepan, melt the butter over low heat, add the onion and cook for 8 minutes. Add the ginger, cinnamon and pepper and stir for 1 minute. Increase the heat to high, add the lamb and stir until the meat changes colour. Reduce the heat, add 375 ml (13 fl oz/1½ cups) of water, along with the chopped dates, saffron and 1 teaspoon of salt. Reduce the heat to low, cover and simmer for 1½ hours, stirring occasionally to prevent the sauce sticking as the dates cook to a purée.

Stir in the honey and lemon juice and adjust the seasoning. Put the unpitted dates on top, cover and simmer for 10 minutes, or until the dates are plump.

Meanwhile, remove and discard the pulp and membranes from the preserved lemon. Rinse the rind under cold running water, then pat dry with paper towel and cut into strips. Melt the extra butter in a small frying pan over medium heat, add the almonds and brown lightly, stirring often, for 5 minutes. Tip immediately onto a plate to prevent burning.

Remove the whole dates from the top of the lamb and set them aside with the almonds. Ladle the meat into a serving dish or tagine and scatter the dates on top, along with the lemon strips and toasted almonds. Serve hot.

SERVES 6

The whole dates are placed on top of the meat so that they remain intact while cooking.

Shlada Hamed bil Besla wal Ma'danous

Fresh Lemon, Onion and Parsley Salad

In Morocco, this salad is served at the beginning of a meal. Its refreshing flavour makes a delicious accompaniment to simple chargrilled fish, prawns or chicken. Try it also with sweet-tasting fish cooked with dates or prunes.

6 lemons
1 small red onion

1 teaspoon caster (superfine) sugar
3 tablespoons chopped flat-leaf (Italian) parsley

Peel the lemons with a sharp knife, making sure that all the pith and fine membranes are removed, to expose the flesh. Cut the lemons into 1 cm (½ in) thick slices and remove the seeds. Dice the lemon slices and put them in a bowl.

Halve the onion, then slice it thinly and add it to the lemon, along with the sugar, chopped parsley and 1 teaspoon salt. Gently toss, then set aside for 10 minutes. When ready to serve, lightly sprinkle with freshly ground black pepper.

SERVES 6–8

Shlada bil Litchine wa Tamra

Orange and Date Salad

A sweet–sour salad that uses two of Morocco's most prolific fruits. Palate-cleansing, it is usually served as an appetizer salad at the beginning of a meal. However, it can also be served as a dessert – omit the mint leaves and dust lightly with cinnamon.

6 sweet oranges
2 teaspoons orange flower water
8 fresh dates, pitted and thinly sliced lengthways

90 g (3 oz/¾ cup) slivered almonds, lightly toasted
small mint leaves, to serve

Cut off the tops and bases of the oranges. Cut the peel off with a sharp knife, removing all traces of pith and cutting through the outer membranes to expose the flesh. Holding the orange over a bowl to catch any juice, segment the oranges by cutting between the visible membranes. Remove the seeds and place the segments in the bowl. Squeeze the remains of the oranges over the bowl to extract all

the juice. Add the orange flower water and stir gently to combine. Cover with plastic wrap and refrigerate until chilled.

Place the orange segments and the juice on a large flat dish and scatter the dates and almonds over the top. Sprinkle the mint leaves over the top. Serve chilled.

SERVES 4–6

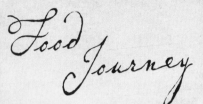

TAGINES

Berber ingenuity created the tagine many centuries ago. Both the pot, and the food cooked in it, are called tagines. Made of earthenware, their colour is determined by the clay available to the potters. Decorative designs are often cut into the clay prior to firing.

The tagine slaoui can be small enough to cook a single serve or large enough to cook for a dozen or more. The dish for cooking is glazed, but the lids are usually unglazed inside and colourfully designed and glazed on the outside, making them decorative without compromising function. During cooking, steam condenses inside the lid and drips back into the food to prevent it from drying out. The knob on the lid is functional; as well as being easy to lift with one hand, while stirring the food with the other, its concave shape makes it an ideal spoon rest. Tagines are also used for storing bread, and the base can be used for serving fresh fruit. Note that for kitchens without a tagine, a baking dish is a good substitute.

In modern city kitchens, food is often cooked in a saucepan or pressure cooker, then served in the tagine, especially if it is fully decorated and glazed. The shallowness of the base is deliberate, so that the food may be accessed easily when eating with the thumb and first two fingers of the right hand in the Moroccan manner. Etiquette dictates that the diner takes food from the section of the tagine that is in front of them. When entertaining, the host might move a tasty morsel to the section of the tagine facing the guest or guests.

Before using a tagine, it must be seasoned, or 'matured', otherwise it could crack when first used. This also serves to remove the earthenware flavour, especially of the unglazed interior of the lid. While this is usually done on a charcoal brazier, an oven is a better option. Check that the tagine fits in the oven, removing the upper shelves. Preheat oven to 150°C (300°F/Gas 2). Wash the new tagine and lid, and wipe dry. To the tagine base, add 1 peeled, roughly chopped onion, 2 roughly chopped carrots, 2 garlic cloves, 1 bay leaf and 2–3 tablespoons olive oil. Almost fill with water. Cover and place in the oven for 40 minutes. Remove and leave at room temperature to cool slowly. Discard the contents, wash the tagine in hot soapy water and then dry it thoroughly.

When cooking in a tagine, it is better to use it over a medium–heat charcoal fire; if using a tagine on a gas fire or an electric hotplate, low heat and a good heat diffuser are recommended; however, tagines are excellent for oven cooking.

Briouat bil Hout

Fried Pastries with Seafood

When making small pastries using filo, the less the pastry is handled the better. Stack the sheets and cut the strips as directed in the method; a craft knife is excellent for cutting through the stack. Avoid using a damp tea towel as it can ruin the filo.

FISH OR PRAWN FILLING
250 g (9 oz) boneless white fish fillets, or 200 g (7 oz)
    cooked prawns (shrimp), peeled and deveined
2 tablespoons finely chopped flat-leaf (Italian) parsley
1 tablespoon finely chopped spring onion (scallion)
1 garlic clove, crushed
1/2 teaspoon paprika
1/4 teaspoon ground cumin
pinch of cayenne pepper

1 tablespoon lemon juice
1 tablespoon olive oil

6 sheets filo pastry
1 egg white, lightly beaten
oil, for deep-frying
3 tablespoons caster (superfine) sugar, to serve
1/8 teaspoon cayenne pepper, to serve
1 teaspoon ground cinnamon, to serve

To make the fish or prawn filling, first poach the fish gently in lightly salted water, to cover, until the flesh flakes – about 4–5 minutes. Remove from the poaching liquid and transfer to a plate. Cover closely with plastic wrap so that the surface does not dry as it cools. When cool, flake the fish. If using cooked prawns, cut them into small pieces. Put the fish or the prawns in a bowl and add the chopped parsley and spring onion, crushed garlic, the paprika, cumin, cayenne pepper, lemon juice and olive oil. Toss well to combine.

Stack the filo sheets on a cutting board, and using a ruler and sharp knife, measure and cut across the width of the pastry to give strips 12 cm (4½ in) wide and 28–30 cm (11¼–12 in) long. Stack the cut filo strips in the folds of a dry tea towel (dish towel) or cover with plastic wrap to prevent them from drying out.

Take a filo strip and, with the narrow end towards you, fold it in half across its width to make a strip 6 cm (2½ in) wide. Place a generous teaspoon of filling 2 cm (3/4 in) in from the base of the strip and fold the end diagonally across the filling so that the base lines up with the side of the strip, forming a triangle. Fold straight up once, then fold diagonally to the opposite side. Continue folding until near the end of the strip, then brush the filo lightly with egg white and complete the fold. Place on a cloth-covered tray, seam-side down. Cover with a tea towel until ready to fry, and cook within 10 minutes.

Heat the oil to 180°C (350°F), or until a cube of bread dropped into the oil browns in 15 seconds. Add four pastries at a time and fry until golden, turning to brown evenly. Remove with a slotted spoon; drain on paper towel. Serve hot with a small bowl of sugar mixed with cayenne and cinnamon.

MAKES 24

MECHOUI

Slow-roasted Lamb with Cumin

This version of mechoui (whole, slow-roasted lamb) uses lamb leg; a forequarter of lamb can be prepared in the same way. While the initial heat is high, the lamb should be cooked in a slow oven and basted frequently to remain moist.

2.25 kg (5 lb) leg of lamb
70 g (2 oz) butter, softened at room temperature
3 garlic cloves, crushed
2 teaspoons ground cumin

3 teaspoons ground coriander
1 teaspoon paprika
1 tablespoon ground cumin, extra, to serve
1½ teaspoons coarse salt, to serve

Preheat the oven to 220°C (425°F/Gas 7). With a small sharp knife, cut small deep slits in the top and sides of the lamb.

Mix the butter, garlic, cumin, coriander paprika and ¼ teaspoon salt in a bowl to form a smooth paste. With the back of a spoon, rub the paste all over the lamb leg, then use your fingers to spread the paste evenly, making sure that all of the lamb is covered.

Put the lamb, bone-side down, in a deep roasting tin and place on the top shelf of the oven. Bake for 10 minutes, then baste with the pan juices and return to the centre shelf of the oven. Reduce the oven to 160°C (315°F/Gas 2–3). Bake the lamb for 3¼ hours, basting it every 20–30 minutes to ensure that it stays tender and flavoursome. Carve the lamb into chunky pieces. Mix the extra cumin with the coarse salt and serve it on the side for sprinkling over.

SERVES 6

ZAALOOK

Warm Eggplant Salad

This chunky cooked salad makes a perfect starter with crusty bread. If your eggplants are glossy, heavy for their size and yield slightly when pressed, these are signs that they are not over-ripe. In this case, you can omit the salting as they are less bitter.

2 x 450 g (1 lb) eggplants (aubergines)
3 tomatoes
olive oil, for frying
2 garlic cloves, finely chopped
1 teaspoon paprika
1/2 teaspoon ground cumin

1/4 teaspoon cayenne pepper, or to taste
2 tablespoons finely chopped coriander (cilantro) leaves
2 1/2 tablespoons lemon juice
1/2 preserved lemon (page 247) or fresh lemon slices, to serve

Using a vegetable peeler, remove 1 cm (1/2 in) wide strips of skin along the length of each eggplant. Cut the eggplants into 1 cm (1/2 in) slices, sprinkle with salt and layer the slices in a colander. Leave for 20–30 minutes, then rinse under cold running water. Drain, squeeze the slices gently, then pat them dry with paper towel.

Meanwhile, peel the tomatoes. To do this, score a cross in the base of each one using a knife. Put the tomatoes in a bowl of boiling water for 20 seconds, then plunge them into a bowl of cold water to cool. Remove the tomatoes from the water and peel the skin away from the cross – it should slip off easily. Cut in half crossways and squeeze out the seeds. Chop the tomatoes and set aside.

Heat the oil in a frying pan to a depth of 5 mm (1/4 in). Fry the eggplant in batches until browned on each side. Add more oil to the pan as needed. Set the eggplant aside on a plate.

Using the oil left in the pan, cook the garlic over low heat for a few seconds. Add the tomatoes, paprika, cumin and cayenne pepper and increase the heat to medium. Add the eggplant and cook, mashing the eggplant and tomato gently with a fork. Continue to cook until most of the liquid has evaporated. When the oil separates, drain off some if it seems excessive; however, some should be left in as it adds to the flavour of the dish. Add the coriander leaves and lemon juice and season with freshly ground black pepper and a little salt if necessary. Transfer to a serving bowl.

If using preserved lemon, rinse under cold running water and remove the pulp and membranes. Finely chop the rind and scatter it over the eggplant or, alternatively, garnish with slices of fresh lemon. Serve warm or at room temperature with bread.

SERVES 6–8

BESTILLA

Festive Chicken Pie

Traditionally, this famous Moroccan pie is made with pigeons, and they are given as an alternative. Squab pigeons are young pigeons specially bred for the table. Chicken is a popular substitute in this dish, even in Morocco.

150 g (6 oz) smen (page 243) or butter
1.5 kg (3 lb 5 oz) chicken, quartered, or
   3 x 500 g (1 lb 2 oz) squab pigeons, halved
2 large red onions, finely chopped
3 garlic cloves, crushed
1 cinnamon stick
1 teaspoon ground ginger
1½ teaspoons ground cumin
¼ teaspoon cayenne pepper
½ teaspoon ground turmeric
pinch of saffron threads soaked in
   2 tablespoons warm water

500 ml (17 fl oz/2 cups) chicken stock
1 tablespoon lemon juice
3 tablespoons chopped flat-leaf (Italian) parsley
3 tablespoons chopped coriander (cilantro) leaves
5 eggs, lightly beaten
100 g (4 oz/²/₃ cup) blanched almonds, toasted
   and finely chopped
3 tablespoons icing (confectioners') sugar,
   plus extra to serve
1 teaspoon ground cinnamon, plus extra to serve
100 g (4 oz) smen (page 243), extra, melted
14 sheets filo pastry

Preheat the oven to 160°C (315°F/Gas 2–3). Melt the smen in a flameproof casserole dish over medium heat. Brown the chicken or squab well, then set aside. Add the onion to the dish and cook for 10 minutes, or until golden. Stir in the garlic and spices, then the saffron, its soaking liquid and the stock. Add the chicken and turn to coat. Cover and bake, turning occasionally, for 1 hour, or until cooked through. Add a little extra water if needed. Remove the chicken, reserving the sauce. Discard the cinnamon stick. Remove the chicken from the bones and cut into small pieces.

Put the sauce, lemon juice and herbs in a saucepan and reduce over high heat for 10 minutes, or until thick. Reduce the heat to very low, gradually stir in the eggs until scrambled, then remove from the heat. Add the chicken, and season, to taste.

Mix the almonds with the icing sugar and cinnamon. Grease a 30 cm (12 in) pizza pan or pie plate with melted smen.

Increase the oven temperature to 180°C (350°F/Gas 4). Stack eight sheets of filo pastry and brush the top sheet with smen. Place that sheet evenly across the pan with the ends overhanging. Repeat with the next seven sheets, brushing and fanning sheets to cover the pan, with the pastry overhanging evenly all round. Fill with the chicken mixture and smooth over. Fold four of the flaps back over, then brush with smen and sprinkle with the almond mixture. Fold the other four sheets over and brush the top with smen. Brush the remaining six filo sheets with smen, fanning onto the pie as before. Using kitchen scissors, cut the overhanging pastry evenly around the edge about 3 cm (1¼ in) from the edge of the pan. Using a rubber spatula to lift up the edge of the pie, tuck the overhanging pastry underneath. Bake the pie for 45–50 minutes, or until golden.

Sift extra icing sugar over the top of the pie and make a lattice pattern with extra cinnamon.

SERVES 6–8

Tagine 'L'ghanmi Be'sfargel

Lamb Tagine with Quince

This sweet–sour dish of lamb with quince and apricots illustrates the early Persian influence in Moroccan cuisine, but the spicing is pure Moroccan. If the flavour is too tart for your liking, add some honey to taste as well as the sugar.

1.5 kg (3 lb 5 oz) lamb shoulder,
  cut into 3 cm (1¼ in) pieces
2 large brown onions, diced
½ teaspoon ground ginger
½ teaspoon cayenne pepper
⅛ teaspoon ground saffron threads
1 teaspoon ground coriander
1 cinnamon stick

3 tablespoons roughly chopped coriander
  (cilantro) leaves
40 g (1½ oz) butter
500 g (1 lb 2 oz) quinces, peeled, cored
  and quartered
100 g (4 oz/½ cup) dried apricots
3 tablespoons caster (superfine) sugar
coriander (cilantro) leaves, extra, to serve

Put the lamb in a large heavy-based, flameproof casserole dish and add half the onion, the ginger, cayenne pepper, saffron, ground coriander, cinnamon stick, chopped coriander and some salt and pepper. Add 375 ml (13 fl oz/1½ cups) water and bring to the boil over medium–high heat. Lower the heat and simmer, covered, for 1 hour.

While the lamb is cooking, melt the butter in a heavy-based frying pan over medium heat and cook the remaining onion and the quinces for

15 minutes, or until lightly golden. Add the quince mixture, apricots and sugar to the lamb and cook for 30 minutes, or until the lamb is tender.

Taste the sauce and adjust the seasoning. Transfer to a warm serving dish and sprinkle with the extra coriander. Serve with couscous or rice.

SERVES 6–8

While quince discolours when cut, this disappears once cooking begins in the butter.

Tafaya

Lamb with Eggs and Almonds

Tafaya is served at celebrations throughout Morocco. To give the dish a festive touch, some cooks dip the shelled, boiled eggs in saffron-infused hot water, which colours them and gives them a special fragrance and flavour.

1.25 kg (2 lb 12 oz) lamb shoulder chops
3 tablespoons olive oil
2 brown onions, coarsely grated
3 garlic cloves, finely chopped
2 teaspoons ground ginger
1/8 teaspoon ground saffron threads

3 tablespoons chopped coriander (cilantro) leaves
40 g (1½ oz) butter
150 g (6 oz/1 cup) blanched almonds
6 hard-boiled eggs
coriander (cilantro) leaves, extra, to serve

Trim the excess fat from the chops. Heat half the olive oil in a large saucepan over high heat and brown the chops on each side in batches, transferring to a dish when cooked. Add a little more oil as required.

Reduce the heat to low, add the remaining olive oil and the onion and cook for 8 minutes, or until softened. Add the garlic and ginger and cook for a few seconds. Pour in 375 ml (13 fl oz/1½ cups) water and stir to lift the browned juices off the base of the pan. Return the lamb chops to the pan, along with the saffron, 1 teaspoon salt and a good grinding of black pepper. Cover and simmer for 1¼ hours, then stir in the coriander and cook for a further 15 minutes, or until the lamb is tender.

Meanwhile, melt the butter in a frying pan over medium heat, add the almonds and fry, tossing frequently, for 5 minutes, or until golden. Remove immediately to a bowl to prevent them burning. Shell and halve the boiled eggs.

Arrange the lamb on a serving dish, spoon the sauce over the top and sprinkle with the almonds (warm the almonds a little first if the butter has congealed). Arrange the egg halves on top and scatter with a few coriander leaves.

SERVES 6

Prepare the lamb chops by trimming off the excess fat with a sharp knife.

Mezghaldi B'besla bil Boudenjal
Caramelized Onions with Chargrilled Eggplants

These spicy, caramelized onions are usually served on their own as an appetizer salad, but they can also be teamed with chargrilled eggplant. This also makes a delicious accompaniment to chargrilled meats or chicken.

4 brown onions
100 ml (4 fl oz) olive oil
1/4 teaspoon ground saffron threads
1 teaspoon ground ginger

1 teaspoon ground cinnamon
1/2 teaspoon allspice
1 1/2 tablespoons honey
600 g (1 lb 5 oz) long thin eggplants (aubergines)

Halve the onions lengthways and cut them into slender wedges. Put them in a frying pan, cover with cold water and bring to the boil. Cover and simmer for 5 minutes. Drain the onion in a colander.

Add 2 tablespoons of the oil to the pan over low heat and stir in the saffron, ginger, cinnamon and allspice. Cook for 1 minute, then increase the heat to medium and return the onion to the pan. Add the honey and 375 ml (13 fl oz/1 1/2 cups) of water. Season with salt and freshly ground black pepper. Stir well, reduce the heat, cover and simmer for 40 minutes. Uncover and simmer for 10 minutes, or until most of the liquid has evaporated.

Wash and dry the eggplants. Leaving the green stalks on for effect, halve them lengthways. Using the remaining oil, brush all the eggplant halves on each side. Cook the eggplants in a heated chargrill pan or on a barbecue grill for 3–4 minutes on each side, or until tender, adjusting the heat so that they do not burn.

Arrange the eggplants, cut-side up, on a platter or individual plates and season lightly with salt. Top with the onion and pour over any juices from the pan. Serve hot or warm with crusty bread.

PICTURE ON PAGE 146

SERVES 4

Right: Select the slender long eggplants so that they are not too thick when halved lengthways.

Far right: Brush the eggplants with the oil, then cook on a chargrill pan or barbecue grill until tender.

Caramelized Onions with Chargrilled Eggplants
(recipe on page 145)

Kseksou Bidawi bil Djej

Couscous with Chicken and Vegetables

This is one of the most frequently prepared couscous dishes in Moroccan households on Fridays – the traditional day for serving couscous. The chicken and the vegetables are served on top of the couscous and moistened with a harissa-flavoured broth.

1.6 kg (3 lb 8 oz) chicken
3 tablespoons smen (page 243) or ghee
1 brown onion, finely chopped
1/2 teaspoon ground turmeric
1/2 teaspoon ground cumin
8 baby onions, trimmed
1/4 teaspoon ground saffron threads
1 cinnamon stick
4 coriander (cilantro) sprigs and 4 flat-leaf (Italian)
    parsley sprigs, tied in a bunch
3 tomatoes, peeled, seeded and chopped

3 carrots, cut into chunks
4 zucchini (courgettes), cut into chunks
200 g (7 oz/1 1/3 cups) shelled green peas,
    or very young broad (fava) beans
420 g (15 oz) tin chickpeas, rinsed and drained
3 tablespoons herbed smen (page 243) or butter
1 quantity couscous (page 244)
3 teaspoons harissa (page 242), or to taste

Joint the chicken into eight pieces, leaving the skin on. Heat the smen in a large saucepan or the base of a large couscoussier, add the chicken and brown on each side. Reduce the heat, add the onion and cook until it has softened. Stir in the turmeric and cumin and add the baby onions.

Pour in 750 ml (26 fl oz/3 cups) water, then add the saffron, cinnamon stick, the bunch of herbs and tomato. Season with 1 1/2 teaspoons salt and freshly ground black pepper, to taste. Bring to a gentle boil, then cover and cook over low heat for 25 minutes. Add the carrot and simmer for a further 20 minutes. Add the zucchini, peas and chickpeas and cook for 20 minutes, or until the chicken and vegetables are tender.

Stir the herbed smen through the hot couscous. Spoon the chicken and vegetables on top of the couscous. Moisten with some of the broth from the stew. Put 250 ml (9 fl oz/1 cup) of the broth into a bowl and stir in the harissa. The harissa-flavoured broth is added, according to individual taste, to the couscous to keep it moist.

SERVES 6–8

DJEJ 'MSHERMEL
Chicken with Preserved Lemon and Olives

One of the classic dishes of Morocco, this combination of subtly spiced chicken, preserved lemon and olives is usually served at banquets. Use unpitted green olives; if bitter, blanch them in boiling water for 5 minutes before adding to the chicken.

¼ preserved lemon (page 247)
3 tablespoons olive oil
1.6 kg (3 lb 8 oz) chicken
1 brown onion, chopped
2 garlic cloves, chopped
625 ml (22 fl oz/2½ cups) chicken stock
½ teaspoon ground ginger

1½ teaspoons ground cinnamon
pinch of saffron threads
100 g (4 oz/½ cup) green olives
2 bay leaves
2 chicken livers
3 tablespoons chopped coriander (cilantro) leaves

Rinse the preserved lemon quarter under cold running water, remove and discard the pulp and membranes. Drain the rind, pat dry with paper towel and cut into strips. Set aside.

Preheat the oven to 180°C (350°F/Gas 4). Heat 2 tablespoons of the oil in a large frying pan, add the chicken and brown all over. Place in a deep baking dish.

Heat the remaining olive oil in the frying pan over medium heat, add the onion and garlic and cook for 5 minutes, or until the onion has softened. Add the stock, ginger, cinnamon, saffron, olives, bay

leaves and preserved lemon strips. Stir well, then pour the sauce around the chicken. Bake, basting the chicken occasionally, for 1½ hours, or until cooked through, adding a little water or stock if the sauce gets too dry.

Remove the chicken from the dish, cover with foil and leave to rest. Pour the contents of the baking dish into a frying pan and place over medium heat. Add the chicken livers and mash into the sauce as they cook. Cook for 5–6 minutes, or until the sauce has reduced and thickened. Stir in the coriander. Carve the chicken into pieces and serve hot with the sauce.

SERVES 4

Brown the chicken in a non-stick frying pan so that the chicken skin remains intact. Use the same pan for completing the sauce after the chicken is cooked.

COQUE BIL FUL
Artichokes with Broad Beans

Globe artichokes and broad beans apppear in the souks at the same time, but the beans are at their best early in the season. Mature broad beans should be skinned before cooking. Watercress substitutes for a wild herb called bakoola.

1 lemon
4 globe artichokes
3 tablespoons olive oil
1 white onion, finely chopped
2 garlic cloves, finely chopped
2 tablespoons chopped flat-leaf (Italian) parsley

2 tablespoons chopped fresh fennel leaves
1 kg (2 lb 4 oz) fresh broad (fava) beans, shelled
1 preserved lemon (page 247)
3 large handfuls cleaned watercress, coarsely chopped
fennel sprigs, or chopped fennel, to serve

Halve the lemon and squeeze the juice of one half into a bowl of cold water. Cut the remainder of the lemon in half and use it to rub the cut surfaces as the artichokes are prepared.

Cut the stem off an artichoke close to base. Cut a 12 cm (4½ in) piece from the top of the stem, discarding the remainder. Pull off and discard four or five layers of outer leaves of artichoke until the base of the remaining leaves are a light yellow–green. Trim carefully around the base where the leaves were removed. Each time you make a new cut or trim, rub the exposed surface with the cut lemon. Cut off and discard the top quarter of the artichoke. Cut the remaining artichoke in half, remove the hairy choke with a teaspoon, cut again to make quarters, then drop into the lemon water. Peel the fibrous layer from the stem, cut in half crossways and add to the bowl. Repeat with the remaining artichokes.

In a large stainless steel or enamelled saucepan, warm the oil over medium heat. Add the onion and cook gently for 5 minutes, or until soft. Add the garlic, cook for a few seconds, then stir in the herbs and drained artichokes and stems. Cook for 2 minutes, then add the broad beans and 750 ml (26 fl oz/3 cups) water. Season and bring to the boil over high heat, then reduce to low–medium and simmer, partly covered, for 15 minutes.

Meanwhile, remove and discard the pulp and membranes from the preserved lemon. Rinse the rind well, cut into strips and reserve one-quarter for garnish. Stir the watercress and the remaining preserved lemon into the artichokes and cook, uncovered, for 10–15 minutes, or until the broad beans and artichokes are tender. Towards the end of cooking, boil rapidly to reduce the liquid by half. Transfer to a shallow dish and sprinkle with the reserved lemon strips and fennel.

SERVES 4–6

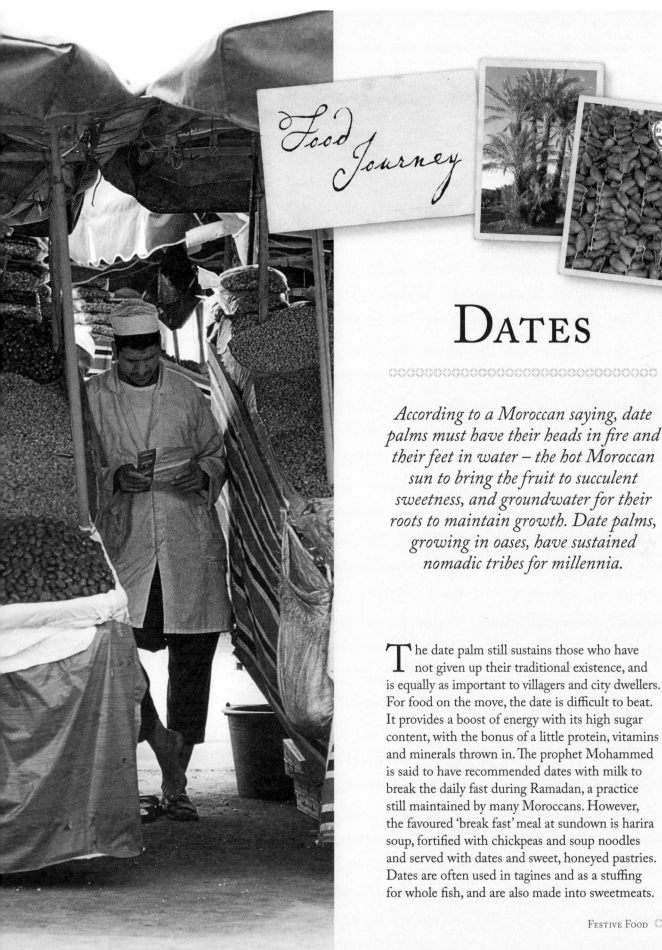

Food Journey

DATES

◇◇◇◇◇◇◇◇◇◇◇◇◇◇◇◇◇◇◇◇◇◇◇◇◇◇◇◇◇◇◇

According to a Moroccan saying, date palms must have their heads in fire and their feet in water – the hot Moroccan sun to bring the fruit to succulent sweetness, and groundwater for their roots to maintain growth. Date palms, growing in oases, have sustained nomadic tribes for millennia.

The date palm still sustains those who have not given up their traditional existence, and is equally as important to villagers and city dwellers. For food on the move, the date is difficult to beat. It provides a boost of energy with its high sugar content, with the bonus of a little protein, vitamins and minerals thrown in. The prophet Mohammed is said to have recommended dates with milk to break the daily fast during Ramadan, a practice still maintained by many Moroccans. However, the favoured 'break fast' meal at sundown is harira soup, fortified with chickpeas and soup noodles and served with dates and sweet, honeyed pastries. Dates are often used in tagines and as a stuffing for whole fish, and are also made into sweetmeats.

Fresh dates take a year to mature, appearing in the souks in December, often arranged painstakingly in mini pyramids. Hues vary from light golden brown, through red-brown to a rich chocolate.

As well as its fruit, the date palm provides fronds, which are dried and used for baskets, table mats and as string; the fibre from its bark is made into ropes; the stones of the fruit are used for fuel; and the trunk provides timber. Date palms can produce fruit for 60 years; however, they can exceed heights of 30 metres (100 feet), so they are cut down when the harvesting becomes too difficult. In the Erfoud oasis, one million date palms flourish, encompassing 30 varieties. The average annual yield is about 45 kg (100 lb) of fruit per tree. Muslims regard the date palm as the tree of life – it is easy to see why.

Dates are found at dried fruit and nut stalls in the souks. These stalls are a useful source for stocking the home pantry, and are heaven for any health-conscious snackers. Besides stocking date varieties, there are raisins, apricots and prunes for cooking and snacking, dried banana slices, almonds, cashew nuts, peanuts in the shell, pumpkin seeds and dried figs strung on dried date-palm fronds.

Djej bil Kseksou
Roast Chicken with Couscous Stuffing

Moroccan cooks usually steam stuffed chicken or cook it whole in a tagine. To brown it, they remove it from its sauce if necessary, and fry it on all sides in a frying pan. The following recipe is for oven-roasted chicken.

1.6 kg (3 lb 8 oz) chicken
2 teaspoons paprika
30 g (1 oz) butter, softened
250 ml (9 fl oz/1 cup) chicken stock

STUFFING
140 g (5 oz/³⁄₄ cup) couscous
40 g (1¹⁄₂ oz/¹⁄₃ cup) raisins
30 g (1 oz) butter, diced
1 tablespoon honey
¹⁄₂ teaspoon ground cinnamon
40 g (1¹⁄₂ oz/¹⁄₄ cup) blanched almonds, lightly toasted

Preheat the oven to 180°C (350°F/Gas 4). Rinse the cavity of the chicken and dry with paper towel. Season the chicken on the outside and sprinkle with paprika. Rub it into the skin.

To prepare the stuffing, put the couscous in a glass or ceramic lidded casserole dish, then mix in the raisins, butter, honey and cinnamon. Pour on 125 ml (4 fl oz/¹⁄₂ cup) boiling water, stir well and set aside until absorbed. Fluff up the grains with a fork to break up the lumps, cover and microwave on full power for 2¹⁄₂ minutes. Fluff up with the fork, then add the almonds and toss through. Alternatively, follow the directions on the packet to prepare the couscous, adding the extra ingredients.

Spoon the stuffing into the cavity of the chicken, packing it in loosely. Tie the legs together and tuck the wing tips under. Reserve the left-over stuffing.

Spread a little of the softened butter in the base of a roasting tin. Put the chicken in the tin, breast-side up, spread with the remaining butter and then pour the stock into the tin. Roast the chicken for 1¹⁄₂–1³⁄₄ hours, basting often with the liquid in the pan. Remove to a platter, cover lightly with foil and rest in a warm place for 15 minutes before carving. The juices left in the roasting tin may be strained over the chicken. Reheat the remaining couscous stuffing and serve with the chicken.

SERVES 4–6

Far left: Once you have spooned the stuffing into the chicken cavity, tie the legs together and tuck the wing tips under.

Left: Rest the cooked chicken before carving.

Shlada bil Khizou wa Litchine

Carrot and Orange Salad

The classic combination of carrot and orange is not confined to Moroccan cuisine. Some cooks juice the oranges, shred the carrots and blend these to a thick purée with the remaining ingredients. It is sipped from small glasses.

3 sweet oranges
500 g (1 lb 2 oz) carrots
2 tablespoons lemon juice
1 teaspoon ground cinnamon, plus extra, to serve

1 tablespoon caster (superfine) sugar
1 tablespoon orange flower water
small mint leaves, to serve

Cut off the tops and bases of the oranges. Cut the peel off with a sharp knife, removing all traces of pith and cutting through the outer membranes to expose the flesh. Holding the orange over a bowl to catch any juice, segment the oranges by cutting between the visible membranes. Remove the seeds and place the segments in the bowl. Squeeze the remains of the orange to extract all the juice. Pour the juice into another bowl.

Peel and julienne the carrots using a sharp knife. Put the carrots in the bowl with the orange juice.

Add the lemon juice, cinnamon, sugar, orange flower water and a small pinch of salt. Stir well to combine. Cover the carrot mixture and oranges and refrigerate until required.

Just before serving, drain off the accumulated juice from the oranges and arrange the segments around the edge of a serving platter. Pile the carrots in the centre, then scatter the mint leaves over the top. Dust the oranges lightly with a little cinnamon.

SERVES 6

Either julienne the carrots with a sharp knife, use a plastic mandolin (vegetable slicer) with a julienne blade, or use a special julienne shredder.

Chapter 4

THE COAST

Baked fish robustly seasoned with herbs, lemon and spices, pies plump with seafood, and kebabs and tagines make the most of the day's catch… always plentiful and dazzlingly fresh and flavoursome.

KEMROOM BIL CHERMOULA

Prawns with Herbs and Preserved Lemon

There are various versions of chermoula. It is used widely in cooking seafood, with the preserved lemon in this version adding a delicate piquancy. If you do not have preserved lemon on hand, add the zest of half a lemon and lemon juice to taste.

1 kg (2 lb 4 oz) raw large prawns (shrimp)
2 tablespoons olive oil
lemon wedges, to serve
saffron rice (page 246), to serve

CHERMOULA
1/2 preserved lemon (page 247)
2 garlic cloves, roughly chopped
3 tablespoons chopped flat-leaf (Italian) parsley

3 tablespoons chopped coriander (cilantro) leaves
1/8 teaspoon ground saffron threads (optional)
1/2 teaspoon paprika
1/8 teaspoon cayenne pepper or
　　1/2 teaspoon harissa (page 242)
1/2 teaspoon ground cumin
2 tablespoons lemon juice
3 tablespoons olive oil

Peel the prawns, leaving the tails intact. To devein the prawns, cut a slit down the back and remove any visible vein. Place the prawns in a colander and rinse under cold water. Shake the colander to remove any excess water. Sprinkle the prawns with 1/2 teaspoon salt, toss through and set aside.

To make the chermoula, remove the pulp and membrane from the preserved lemon, rinse the rind and pat dry with paper towel. Chop roughly and place in a food processor bowl, along with the garlic, parsley, coriander, saffron (if using),

paprika, cayenne pepper, cumin and lemon juice. Process to a coarse paste, gradually adding the olive oil while processing.

Heat the oil in a large frying pan over medium–high heat, then add the prawns and cook, stirring often, until they begin to turn pink. Reduce the heat to medium, add the chermoula and continue to cook, stirring often, for 3 minutes, or until the prawns are firm. Season to taste. Serve hot with lemon wedges and saffron rice.

SERVES 4

In a frying pan, cook the prawns in olive oil, stirring or tossing often, until they stiffen and change colour.

Hout bil Harissa wal Matisha
Baked Fish with Harissa and Tomatoes

The onions placed in the base of the roasting dish not only add flavour, they also prevent the fish from sticking. The Moroccan method of eating with one's fingers comes into its own when a whole fish is served – it is easy to feel the bones!

1 kg (2 lb 4 oz) whole white-fleshed fish, such as
  snapper or bream, scaled and cleaned
3 garlic cloves, crushed
2 teaspoons harissa (page 242), or to taste
2 tablespoons olive oil

1 lemon, thinly sliced
1 brown onion, thinly sliced
2 large firm, ripe tomatoes, sliced
4 thyme sprigs, plus extra for garnish (optional)

Preheat the oven to 200°C (400°F/Gas 6). Lightly grease a large baking dish. Make three diagonal cuts on each side of the fish through the thickest part of the flesh to ensure even cooking.

Combine the garlic, harissa and olive oil in a small dish. Put 2 teaspoons of the harissa mixture inside the fish cavity and spread the remainder over both sides of the fish, rubbing it into the slits. Place two lemon slices in the cavity of the fish.

Arrange the onion slices in a layer in the baking dish. Top with the tomato slices, thyme sprigs and the remaining lemon slices. Place the fish on top and bake, uncovered, for about 25–30 minutes, or until the fish flakes at the thickest part when it is tested with a fork.

Transfer the onion and tomato to a serving dish. Place the fish on top and season with salt. Garnish with extra thyme if desired.

SERVES 4

HOUT BENOUA

Almond-crusted Fish with Prunes

Normally this recipe uses whole fish stuffed with prunes, coated with a ground almond mixture and baked. Fish pieces pan-fried works just as well providing care is taken that the crust does not burn.

4 x 200 g (7 oz) firm white fish fillets, such as Blue Eye, snapper, hake or sea bass
24 pitted prunes
24 blanched almonds, lightly toasted
30 g (1 oz) butter
2 brown onions, sliced
3/4 teaspoon ground ginger
3/4 teaspoon ground cinnamon
1/8 teaspoon freshly ground black pepper

1/8 teaspoon ground saffron threads
1 1/2 teaspoons caster (superfine) sugar
3 teaspoons lemon juice
3 teaspoons orange flower water
1 egg
100 g (4 oz/1 cup) ground almonds
4 tablespoons smen (page 243) or ghee
lemon wedges, to serve

Choose centre-cut fish fillets no more than 3 cm (1 1/4 in) thick at the thickest part. Remove the skin (if present) and season lightly with salt. Cover and refrigerate until you are ready to use. Stuff each prune with a whole toasted almond and set aside.

Melt the butter in a frying pan and add the onion. Cook for 10 minutes over low heat, stirring often, until the onion is soft and golden. Add 1/2 teaspoon each of the ground ginger and cinnamon, a pinch of salt and the black pepper. Stir for 30 seconds, or until fragrant. Pour in 250 ml (9 fl oz/1 cup) water and stir in the saffron. Cover and simmer gently for 5 minutes, then gently stir in the stuffed prunes, sugar, lemon juice and orange flower water and stir gently. Cover and simmer for 15 minutes, or until the prunes are plump.

Meanwhile, beat the egg in a shallow dish with 1/4 teaspoon each of ground ginger, cinnamon and salt. Spread the ground almonds in a flat dish.

Dip the fish into the beaten egg, drain briefly, and coat on all sides with the ground almonds. Place on a tray lined with baking paper.

Melt the smen in a large non-stick frying pan over medium–high heat (the depth of the smen should be about 5 mm/1/4 in). Add the coated fish, reduce the heat to medium and cook for 2 minutes, then turn and cook for another 2 minutes, or until the fish is golden and just cooked through. Do not allow the almond coating to burn. If you have to remove the fish before it is cooked through, place it on top of the prune mixture, cover and simmer gently for 2–3 minutes, taking care that the coating does not become too moist on top. Serve the fish immediately with the onion and prune sauce, with lemon wedges to squeeze over the fish.

SERVES 4

Bouzrouq

Mussels in Tomato Chermoula Sauce

In coastal towns and cities, mussels are usually enjoyed in restaurants rather than at home. The tomato chermoula is a perfect sauce in which to cook them. Serve with plenty of bread to soak up the delicious juices.

2 kg (4 lb 8 oz) large fresh mussels
3 ripe tomatoes
½ preserved lemon (page 247), chopped
3 tablespoons olive oil
1 large brown onion, finely chopped
2 garlic cloves, finely chopped
1 teaspoon ground cumin

1 teaspoon paprika
⅛ teaspoon cayenne pepper
2 tablespoons chopped flat-leaf (Italian) parsley
2 tablespoons chopped coriander (cilantro) leaves
1 tablespoon lemon juice
coriander (cilantro) leaves, extra, for serving

Scrub the mussels and beard them if necessary. If any are open, tap them on your bench, and if they don't close, discard. Refrigerate until ready to use.

To peel the tomatoes, score a cross in the base of each one. Place them in a bowl of boiling water for 20 seconds, then drain and cover with cold water. Drain again, peel the skin away from the cross, halve them crossways and squeeze out the seeds. To prepare the preserved lemon, remove the pulp and membranes. Rinse the rind and chop into small pieces.

In a large pot, heat the oil, add the onion and cook over medium heat for 5 minutes, or until soft. Add the garlic, cumin, paprika and cayenne pepper and cooking, stirring, for 1 minute. Add the tomatoes, herbs and preserved lemon. Season, then cover and simmer for 15 minutes, or until the tomatoes are soft. Add the lemon juice.

Add the mussels, cover the pot tightly and cook over high heat, shaking the pan occasionally, until they open – this should take about 6–8 minutes. Divide the mussels and sauce into bowls. If any mussels have not opened, return them to the pot with a little of the sauce, cover and cook a little longer – if they still do not open, discard them. Sprinkle the mussels with the coriander leaves and serve hot.

PICTURE ON PAGE 170

SERVES 6

Right: Clean the mussels by scrubbing them and removing the beards if necessary.

Far right: Simmer the sauce until the tomatoes are soft before adding the mussels.

Mussels in Tomato Chermoula Sauce
(recipe on page 169)

Chorba bil Hout

Fish Soup

With such a variety of fish available, it is surprising that there are so few fish soup recipes in Moroccan cooking. This soup is typical of the cuisine in Tetuan, in the country's north, where Spanish influences still prevail.

2 red capsicums (peppers)
1 long red chilli
2 tablespoons extra virgin olive oil
1 brown onion, finely chopped
1 tablespoon tomato paste (concentrated purée)
2–3 teaspoons harissa (page 242), to taste
4 garlic cloves, finely chopped

2 teaspoons ground cumin
750 ml (26 fl oz/3 cups) fish stock (page 246)
400 g (14 oz) tin chopped tomatoes
750 g (1 lb 10 oz) boneless firm white fish fillets, cut into 2 cm (3/4 in) cubes
2 bay leaves
2 tablespoons chopped coriander (cilantro) leaves

Cut the capsicums into quarters and remove the membrane and seeds. Cut the chilli in half and remove the seeds. Place the capsicum and chilli, skin-side up, under a grill (broiler) and cook until the skin blackens. Remove and place in a plastic bag, tuck the end of the bag underneath and leave to steam in the bag until cool enough to handle. Remove the blackened skin from the capsicum and the chilli and cut into thin strips. Set aside.

Heat the oil in a large saucepan and cook the onion for 5 minutes, or until softened. Add the tomato paste, harissa, garlic, cumin and 125 ml (4 fl oz/1/2 cup) water, then stir to combine. Add the stock, tomato and 500 ml (17 fl oz/2 cups) water. Bring to the boil, then reduce the heat and add the fish and bay leaves. Simmer for 8 minutes, or until the fish is cooked through and opaque.

Remove the fish with a slotted spoon and set aside. Discard the bay leaves. When the soup has cooled slightly, add half the coriander. Purée in a blender until smooth, or use a stick blender in the pan. Season with salt and freshly ground black pepper.

Return the soup to the pan if necessary, add the fish, capsicum and chilli and gently reheat. Season to taste. Garnish with the remaining coriander and serve hot with crusty bread.

SERVES 6

Use a slotted spoon to remove the cooked fish before puréeing the soup.

Hout bil Harissa wa Zitoun
Fish with Harissa and Olives

The spicy tomato sauce in this recipe takes on a bite with the addition of harissa – add with caution if you have not used it before. An alternative is to add one teaspoon of finely chopped red chilli or a pinch of cayenne pepper.

80 ml (3 fl oz/⅓ cup) olive oil
4 firm white fish fillets, such as Blue Eye,
   snapper or sea perch
seasoned plain (all-purpose) flour, to dust
1 brown onion, chopped
2 garlic cloves, crushed
400 g (14 oz) tin chopped tomatoes

2 teaspoons harissa (page 242), or to taste
2 bay leaves
1 cinnamon stick
185 g (7 oz/1 cup) black olives
1 tablespoon lemon juice
2 tablespoons chopped flat-leaf (Italian) parsley

Heat half the olive oil in a heavy-based frying pan. Dust the fish fillets with the flour and cook over medium heat for 2 minutes on each side, or until golden. Transfer to a plate.

Add the remaining olive oil to the frying pan and cook the onion and garlic for 5 minutes, or until softened. Add the chopped tomatoes, harissa, bay leaves and cinnamon stick. Cook for 10 minutes, or until the sauce has thickened. Season, to taste.

Return the fish to the pan, along with the olives. Spoon the sauce over the fish. Discard the bay leaves and cinnamon stick. Cook for 2 minutes, or until the fish flakes easily with a fork. Add the lemon juice and parsley, and serve hot.

SERVES 4

Coat the fish with flour and fry quickly in olive oil until golden on both sides.

Quotban del Ton bil Chermoula
Tuna Skewers with Herb Marinade

Tuna is ideal for skewers as it is a firm-fleshed fish and does not fall apart during cooking. The chermoula gives the tuna a flavour boost and keeps it moist. While Moroccans cook tuna thoroughly, you can sear it and serve rare if desired.

800 g (1 lb 12 oz) tuna steaks, cut into
   3 cm (1¼ in) cubes
2 tablespoons olive oil
½ teaspoon ground cumin
2 teaspoons finely grated lemon zest

CHERMOULA
3 teaspoons ground cumin
½ teaspoon ground coriander

2 teaspoons paprika
pinch of cayenne pepper
4 garlic cloves, crushed
3 tablespoons chopped flat-leaf (Italian) parsley
3 tablespoons chopped coriander (cilantro) leaves
80 ml (3 fl oz/⅓ cup) lemon juice
125 ml (4 fl oz/½ cup) olive oil

Soak eight bamboo skewers in water for 2 hours, or use metal skewers.

Put the tuna in a shallow non-metallic dish. Combine the olive oil, cumin and lemon zest and pour over the tuna. Toss to coat, then cover and marinate in the refrigerator for 10 minutes only.

Meanwhile, to make the chermoula, put the cumin, coriander, paprika and cayenne pepper in a small frying pan. Cook over medium heat for 30 seconds, or until fragrant. Combine with the remaining chermoula ingredients and set aside.

Thread the tuna onto the skewers. Lightly oil a chargrill pan or barbecue grill. Cook the skewers for 1 minute on each side for rare, or 2 minutes each side for medium. Serve with the chermoula drizzled over the tuna.

SERVES 4

Thread the marinated fish onto soaked bamboo skewers prior to cooking on a chargrill pan or barbecue grill.

Latrwit bil Tamra

Trout Stuffed with Dates

The marriage of dates with fish is a time-honoured practice in Morocco. Traditionally the stuffed fish would be cooked in a tagine, but with domestic ovens now more widely available, it is often oven-baked. The foil wrapping keeps the fish moist.

4 medium-sized trout, scaled and cleaned
140 g (5 oz/³⁄₄ cup) pitted, chopped dried dates
40 g (1¹⁄₂ oz/¹⁄₄ cup) cooked rice
4 tablespoons chopped coriander (cilantro) leaves
¹⁄₄ teaspoon ground ginger
¹⁄₄ teaspoon ground cinnamon
50 g (2 oz/¹⁄₃ cup) roughly chopped blanched almonds
1 white onion, finely chopped
40 g (1¹⁄₂ oz) butter, softened
ground cinnamon, to serve (optional)

Preheat the oven to 180°C (350°F/Gas 4). Rinse the trout under cold running water and pat them dry with paper towel. Season lightly with salt and freshly ground black pepper.

Combine the dates, cooked rice, coriander, ginger, cinnamon, almonds, half the onion and half the butter in a bowl to make the stuffing. Season well with salt and freshly ground black pepper.

Spoon the stuffing into the fish cavities and place each fish on a well-greased double sheet of foil. Brush the fish with the remaining butter, season with salt and freshly ground black pepper and divide the remaining onion among the parcels. Wrap the fish neatly and seal the edges. Bake the parcels on a large baking tray for 15–20 minutes, or until the flesh is opaque and flakes easily with a fork. If desired, serve dusted with cinnamon.

SERVES 4

Spoon the stuffing into the fish cavities before sealing in foil panels to keep the fish moist during cooking.

BESTILLA BEL HOUT

Seafood Pie

The famed bestilla can also be made with a seafood filling, and many recipes exist. The egg yolks in this version are used to thicken the sauce, making a moist filling full of flavours that complement seafoods. Garnish with cooked prawns if desired.

3 tablespoons olive oil
1 large white onion, finely chopped
2 garlic cloves, finely chopped
1 teaspoon ground ginger
1 teaspoon ground turmeric
1/4 teaspoon cayenne pepper
3 tablespoons chopped flat-leaf (Italian) parsley
3 tablespoons chopped coriander (cilantro) leaves
1/2 preserved lemon (page 247), chopped
1 kg (2 lb 4 oz) fish fillets, such as Blue Eye,
   sea bass or ling

250 g (9 oz) cooked prawns (shrimp),
   peeled and deveined
375 ml (13 fl oz/1 1/2 cups) fish stock (page 246)
pinch of pounded saffron threads
2 tablespoons lemon juice
6 egg yolks
125 g (5 oz/1/2 cup) smen (page 243)
   or ghee, melted
11 sheets filo pastry
lemon wedges, for serving

Heat the olive oil in a saucepan over medium–low heat, add the onion and cook for 7–8 minutes, or until very soft. Add the garlic, ginger, turmeric and cayenne pepper. Cook, stirring, for 1 minute, then stir in the chopped parsley, coriander and preserved lemon. Place the fish on top, cover and cook for 10 minutes, or until the flesh is opaque and flakes easily with a fork. Remove the fish. When cool enough to handle, break the fish into small chunks, removing any skin and bones. Cut the prawns into pieces if large; add to the fish, cover and set aside.

Meanwhile, add the fish stock, saffron and lemon juice to the pan and boil gently, uncovered, for a further 15 minutes to develop the flavours. Whisk the egg yolks in a bowl, beat in half the hot liquid from the pan, then pour back into the pan. Stir constantly over low heat until the sauce is thick and coats the back of a wooden spoon. Stir in the fish and prawns and season if necessary. Set aside to cool to room temperature.

Preheat the oven to 180°C (350°F/Gas 4). Grease a 30 cm (12 in) pizza pan with melted smen.

Stack six sheets of filo pastry and brush the top sheet with smen. Place evenly across the pan with the ends overhanging. Repeat with the remaining sheets, fanning them out to cover the pan, with pastry overhanging evenly all round. Spread the fish filling in the pan and fold the pastry overhang over the filling. Brush with smen, then brush the remaining pastry with smen and place on the pie, fanning them out as before. Do not brush the last sheet of filo.

With kitchen scissors, cut the pastry evenly around the edge, about 3 cm (1 1/4 in) from the edge of the pan. Using a rubber spatula, lift the edge of the pie and tuck the overhang underneath. Brush the top with smen and bake for 40 minutes, or until the pie is golden. Serve with lemon wedges.

SERVES 6

Hout Tungera

Fish Tagine with Tomato and Potato

When cooking fish in a tagine, Moroccan cooks prevent it from sticking to the base of the tagine by using crisscrossed bamboo canes, pieces of celery or sticks of carrot. Potato slices serve the same purpose, and become a delicious part of the dish.

CHERMOULA
2 garlic cloves, roughly chopped
3 tablespoons chopped flat-leaf (Italian) parsley
3 tablespoons chopped coriander (cilantro) leaves
2 teaspoons paprika
2 teaspoons ground cumin
1/4 teaspoon cayenne pepper
1 tablespoon lemon juice
2 tablespoons olive oil

4 x 2 cm (3/4 in) thick firm white fish steaks,
    such as snapper or Blue Eye
500 g (1 lb 2 oz) potatoes
375 g (13 oz) ripe tomatoes
1 green capsicum (pepper)
1 1/2 tablespoons tomato paste (concentrated purée)
1 teaspoon caster (superfine) sugar
1 tablespoon lemon juice
2 tablespoons olive oil
2 tablespoons combined chopped flat-leaf (Italian)
    parsley and coriander (cilantro) leaves

To make the chermoula, pound the garlic to a paste with 1/2 teaspoon salt using a mortar and pestle. Add the parsley, coriander, paprika, cumin, cayenne pepper and the lemon juice. Pound the mixture to a rough paste, then work in the oil.

Rub half the chermoula on each side of the fish, place the fish in a dish, then cover and set aside for 20 minutes.

Cut the potatoes and tomatoes into 5 mm (1/4 in) thick slices. Remove the seeds and membrane from the capsicum and cut into 5 mm (1/4 in) thick strips.

Preheat the oven to 200°C (400°F/Gas 6). Brush a 30 x 40 x 6 cm (12 x 16 x 2 1/2 in) ovenproof dish with oil. Place a layer of potato slices in the bottom of the dish. Put the fish on top. Toss the remaining potato slices with the remaining chermoula and arrange over the fish. Top with the tomato slices and capsicum strips. Mix the tomato paste with 125 ml (4 fl oz/1/2 cup) water and add 1/2 teaspoon salt, a good grinding of black pepper, the sugar, lemon juice and olive oil. Pour over the fish and sprinkle with the mixed herbs.

Cover the dish with foil and bake for 40 minutes, then remove the foil and move the dish to the top shelf. Cook for a further 10 minutes, or until the fish and potato are tender and the top is lightly crusted. Serve hot.

SERVES 4

Kemroon M'hammar

Spicy Prawns

M'hammar is one of the four basic flavouring combinations of Moroccan cuisine, with its main ingredients being garlic, paprika and cumin. With the addition of red chilli, this prawn dish is a worthy rival to the popular garlic prawns.

375 g (13 oz) raw prawns (shrimp)
3 tablespoons olive oil
½ teaspoon ground cumin
½ teaspoon cumin seeds
1 teaspoon ground ginger
2 teaspoons chopped red chilli

3 garlic cloves, finely chopped
½ teaspoon ground turmeric
1 teaspoon paprika
2 tablespoons finely chopped coriander (cilantro) leaves
lemon wedges, to serve

Peel the prawns, leaving the tails intact. To devein the prawns, cut a slit down the back and remove any visible vein. Put the prawns in a colander and rinse under cold running water. Shake the colander to remove any excess water, sprinkle the prawns with ½ teaspoon salt, toss through and set aside.

Heat the oil in a large frying pan over medium heat. Stir in the ground cumin, cumin seeds, ginger and red chilli. Cook until fragrant and the cumin

seeds start to pop, then add the garlic, turmeric and paprika. Cook, stirring, for a few seconds, then add the prawns. Increase the heat a little and cook the prawns, tossing frequently, for 3–4 minutes, or until they firm up and turn pink.

Stir in the chopped coriander and 3 tablespoons water and bring to a simmer. Remove from the heat. Serve immediately with lemon wedges.

SERVES 4

To devein prawns, cut a shallow slit along the back to expose the visible vein and pull it out gently.

SARDIN MRAQAD

Fried Sardine Sandwiches

Sardines are at their best when sandwiched with a filling of chermoula. Some fish merchants split and fillet them, cutting off the tails, but it is easy to do this yourself and you can even leave the tails on for effect if desired.

24 fresh sardines
olive oil, for frying
plain (all-purpose) flour, to dust
lemon wedges, to serve

CHERMOULA STUFFING
1 tablespoon drained grated white onion
1 garlic clove, crushed
3 tablespoons finely chopped flat-leaf (Italian) parsley

3 tablespoons finely chopped coriander (cilantro) leaves
1/4 teaspoon cayenne pepper
1/2 teaspoon paprika
1/4 teaspoon freshly ground black pepper
1/2 teaspoon ground cumin
1/2 teaspoon grated lemon zest
2 teaspoons lemon juice
2 teaspoons olive oil

To butterfly the sardines, first remove the heads. Cut through the undersides of the sardines and rinse under cold water. Snip the backbone at the tail with kitchen scissors, without cutting through the skin, and pull carefully away from the body, starting from the tail end. Open out the sardines and pat the inside surface dry with paper towel. Sprinkle lightly with salt. Set aside.

To make the stuffing, put the drained onion in a bowl and add the garlic, parsley, coriander, cayenne pepper, paprika, black pepper, cumin, lemon zest, lemon juice and olive oil. Mix well.

Place 12 sardines on a work surface, skin-side down. Spread the stuffing on each sardine and then cover with another sardine, skin-side up. Press them firmly together.

Heat the olive oil to a depth of 5 mm (1/4 in) in a large frying pan. Dust the sardines with flour and fry in the hot oil for 2 minutes on each side, or until crisp and evenly browned. Serve hot with lemon wedges.

SERVES 6 AS AN APPETIZER

Far left: Spread chermoula on a butterflied sardine, then top with another butterflied sardine and press firmly together.

Left: The sandwiched sardines are floured, then fried in olive oil and served hot.

Kseksou bel Hout

Fish Couscous

In seaside towns, the Friday couscous is more than likely to use fish as the main ingredient rather than lamb or chicken. This is a simple couscous to make, typically herbed and spiced, with rich red tomatoes adding colour and flavour.

750 g (1 lb 10 oz) firm white fish fillets,
    such as snapper, hake or sea bass
3 tablespoons plain (all-purpose) flour
olive oil, for frying
1 large brown onion, finely chopped
2 garlic cloves, finely chopped
½ teaspoon ground cumin
1 teaspoon paprika
¼ teaspoon cayenne pepper

400 g (14 oz) tin chopped tomatoes
125 ml (4 fl oz/½ cup) fish stock (page 246)
1 tablespoon fresh thyme leaves
2 tablespoons chopped flat-leaf (Italian) parsley
2 tablespoons chopped coriander (cilantro) leaves
pinch of saffron threads
60 g (2 oz) unsalted butter
1 quantity couscous (page 244)

Cut the fish into 4 cm (1½ in) pieces. Heat the oil to a depth of 5 mm (¼ in) in a large lidded frying pan over medium–high heat. Coat the fish pieces with flour and fry in the hot oil, turning to brown each side. The fish need not be cooked through. Transfer to a plate.

Discard the frying oil and wipe the pan with paper towel. Add 3 tablespoons oil to the pan and cook the onion over medium heat for 5 minutes, or until soft. Add the chopped garlic, cumin, paprika and cayenne pepper and cook for 1 minute. Add the tomatoes, fish stock, thyme, parsley and coriander. Using a pestle and mortar, pound the saffron with ¼ teaspoon salt, stir into the sauce and season if necessary. Cover and simmer for 20 minutes.

Add the fish and simmer, covered, for 10 minutes, or until the fish flakes easily with a fork.

Toss the butter through the hot couscous. Spoon the fish and sauce over the couscous. Serve hot.

PICTURE ON PAGE 188

SERVES 4

Use a firm white fish such as snapper, hake or sea bass.
Cut the fish into pieces to flour and fry.

Fish Couscous (recipe on page 187)

Hout Za'faran bil Marak Matisha
Saffron Fish Balls in Tomato Sauce

This recipe was devised by Moroccan Jews, who were also the principal gatherers of the saffron crocus when it was introduced from Moorish Spain. It is based on their traditional recipe for fish balls, but with distinctive Moroccan flavours.

500 g (1 lb 2 oz) boneless firm white fish fillets
1 egg
2 spring onions (scallions), chopped
1 tablespoon chopped flat-leaf (Italian) parsley
1 tablespoon chopped coriander (cilantro) leaves
55 g (2 oz/²⁄₃ cup) fresh breadcrumbs
small pinch saffron threads

TOMATO SAUCE
500 g (1 lb 2 oz) tomatoes
1 brown onion, coarsely grated
3 tablespoons olive oil
2 garlic cloves, finely chopped
1 teaspoon paprika
¹⁄₂ teaspoon harissa (page 242), or to taste,
    or ¹⁄₄ teaspoon cayenne pepper
¹⁄₂ teaspoon ground cumin
1 teaspoon caster (superfine) sugar

Roughly chop the fish and put in a food processor bowl, along with the egg, spring onion, herbs and breadcrumbs. Soak the saffron in 1 tablespoon warm water for 5 minutes, then add to the fish mixture with ³⁄₄ teaspoon salt and some freshly ground black pepper. Process to a thick paste, scraping down the side of the bowl occasionally.

With moistened hands, shape the fish mixture into balls the size of a walnut. Put on a tray, cover and set aside in the refrigerator.

To make the tomato sauce, first peel the tomatoes by scoring a cross in the base of each. Put them in a bowl of boiling water for 20 seconds, then plunge into a bowl of cold water to cool. Remove them from the water and peel the skin away from the cross – it should slip off easily. Halve crossways, squeeze out the seeds and chop the flesh.

Put the onion and olive oil in a saucepan and cook over medium heat for 5 minutes. Add the garlic, paprika, harissa and cumin. Stir for a few seconds, then add the tomato, sugar, 250 ml (9 fl oz/1 cup) water, and salt and freshly ground black pepper, to taste. Bring to the boil, then cover, reduce heat and simmer for 15 minutes.

Add the fish balls to the tomato sauce, shaking the pan occasionally as they are added so that they settle into the sauce. Return to a gentle boil over medium heat, then cover, reduce the heat to low and simmer for 20 minutes. Serve the fish balls hot with crusty bread.

SERVES 4

Chapter 5

SWEET DELIGHTS

Fruit and almonds, rosewater, dates and figs feature large in desserts and sweet pastries, along with cinnamon, lemon zest and a drizzle of honey. Mint tea and milk-based sharbats are among the refreshing beverages.

GHORIBA DIAL JANJLANE
Sesame Cookies

Sesame seeds star in these delicious biscuits. Their nutty flavour is accentuated when roasted, but take care that the seeds do not burn. They can be bought from patisseries in the cities, to be taken home or to a nearby café to enjoy with mint tea or coffee.

225 g (8 oz/1½ cups) sesame seeds
150 g (5½ oz/1¼ cups) plain (all-purpose) flour, sifted
165 g (5¾ oz/¾ cup) caster (superfine) sugar
1½ teaspoons baking powder

2 eggs, beaten
1 tablespoon orange flower water
2–3 tablespoons sesame seeds, extra

Put the sesame seeds in a heavy-based saucepan and stir constantly over medium heat for about 7 minutes, or until golden. Tip them immediately into a bowl and leave to cool. Put the flour in the same saucepan, stir constantly over medium heat for about 5 minutes, or until lightly golden, then transfer immediately to a separate mixing bowl.

When the sesame seeds are cool, put them in a blender and process until they are reduced almost to a powder (this is best done in two batches as it is difficult to process the seeds efficiently in one batch). Some seeds should remain visible after processing. Add to the flour, along with the sugar and baking powder and mix thoroughly. Make a well in the centre and add the beaten eggs and orange flower water. Stir into the dry ingredients, then knead well until smooth.

Preheat the oven to 180°C (350°F/Gas 4). Line two baking trays with baking paper or grease them well with butter. Put the extra sesame seeds in a shallow dish.

Break off pieces of dough the size of walnuts and roll them into balls, oiling your hands lightly to prevent the dough sticking. Press the balls in the extra sesame seeds and flatten slightly. Lift carefully so that the topping is not disturbed and place on the baking trays, spacing them 5 cm (2 in) apart to allow for spreading. Bake for 15–20 minutes, or until golden. Leave on the trays for 10 minutes before transferring to a wire rack to cool. Store in an airtight container.

MAKES ABOUT 36

Toast the sesame seeds in a heavy-based pan for even heat distribution, stirring often, then tip immediately into a bowl to prevent the seeds from burning.

'ASSEL DDWAZ DATAY
Fried Honey Cakes

While yeast doughs are usually prepared for sweets such as these delicious honey cakes, here eggs and baking powder are used to give the desired lightness without the need for lengthy kneading of the dough.

3 eggs
3 tablespoons orange juice
3 tablespoons vegetable oil
1 tablespoon grated orange zest
60 g (2¼ oz/¼ cup) caster (superfine) sugar
300 g (10½ oz/2½ cups) plain (all-purpose) flour
1 teaspoon baking powder
about 4 tablespoons plain (all-purpose) flour, extra
vegetable oil, for deep-frying

SYRUP
2 tablespoons lemon juice
275 g (10 oz/1¼ cups) caster (superfine) sugar
115 g (4 oz/⅓ cup) honey
1 tablespoon grated orange zest

Whisk the eggs, orange juice and oil together in a large bowl. Add the orange zest and caster sugar and whisk until frothy. Sift in the flour and baking powder and mix with a wooden spoon until it is smooth, but still a little sticky.

To make the syrup, put 310 ml (10¾ fl oz/1¼ cups) cold water, the lemon juice and sugar in a saucepan and heat, stirring until the sugar dissolves. Bring to the boil, reduce the heat and simmer for 5 minutes. Add the honey and orange zest and then simmer for another 5 minutes. Keep warm.

Sprinkle a little of the extra flour onto the dough and transfer it to a lightly floured surface. Work in just enough extra flour to give a dough that doesn't stick to your hands. Roll out to a thickness of 5 mm (¼ in). It will be very elastic, so keep rolling and resting it until it stops shrinking. Using a 5 cm (2 in) biscuit cutter, cut out round cakes.

Heat the oil in a large deep-sided frying pan to 170°C (325°F), or until a cube of bread dropped into the oil browns in 20 seconds. Fry the cakes three or four at a time for 1 minute on each side, or until puffed and golden. Remove with tongs and drain on paper towel.

Using tongs, dip each cake into the warm honey syrup, long enough for it to soak in. Transfer to a platter. Serve warm or cold.

SERVES 4–6

Briouat B'looz W'assel

Honey-dipped Briouats with Almond Paste

These crisp, honey-dipped pastries are filled with a delicious almond paste fragrant with orange flower water. When boiling honey for dipping, it is important to add water otherwise the honey burns.

ALMOND FILLING
200 g (7 oz/2 cups) ground almonds
60 g (2 oz) unsalted butter
60 g (2 oz/½ cup) icing (confectioners') sugar
¼ teaspoon natural almond extract
1 tablespoon orange flower water

6 sheets filo pastry
125 g (5 oz) smen (page 243), melted

HONEY SYRUP
260 g (9¼ oz/¾ cup) honey
1 tablespoon orange flower water

Place a heavy-based saucepan over medium heat, add the ground almonds and stir constantly until lightly toasted – about 3–4 minutes. Quickly tip into a bowl, add the butter and stir until it melts. When cool, add the icing sugar, almond extract and orange flower water and mix thoroughly to a paste.

Stack the filo pastry on a cutting board with the longer side in front of you and, using a ruler and sharp knife, measure and cut into strips 12–14 cm (4½–5½ in) wide and 28–30 cm (11¼–12 in) long. Stack the strips and cover with a dry, folded cloth to prevent them from drying out.

Place a filo strip on a work surface, brush half the width with smen and fold in half to give a strip about 6 cm (2½ in) wide. Brush over the top with smen and place a heaped teaspoon of the almond filling towards the end of the strip. Fold the end diagonally across the filling so that the base lines up with the side of the strip, forming a triangle.

Fold straight up once, then fold diagonally to the opposite side. Continue to the end of the strip, trimming the excess pastry with scissors. Place, seam-side down, on a lightly greased baking tray. Repeat with the remaining ingredients and brush the tops lightly with smen.

Preheat the oven to 180°C (350°F/Gas 4); do this after the triangles are completed so the kitchen remains cool while shaping. Bake the pastries for 20–25 minutes, or until puffed and golden.

Towards the end of cooking, combine the honey, orange flower water and ¼ cup (60 ml/2 fl oz) of water in a 1.5 litre (52 fl oz/6 cup) saucepan. Bring to the boil, then reduce the heat to low. Dip the hot pastries, two at a time, in the syrup for 20 seconds. Remove with two forks and place on a tray lined with baking paper. As the pastries are dipped, the honey boils up in the pan, so take care. Cool and serve on the day of baking.

MAKES 18

Hleeb B'looz
Almond Milk Drink

There are two versions of almond drink – one containing milk and the other using water only (sharbat b'looz). Traditionally, the almonds are pulverized with sugar in a mortar, but a blender makes the process easier.

235 g (9 oz/1½ cups) fresh blanched almonds
55 g (2 oz/¼ cup) caster (superfine) sugar, or to taste
¼ teaspoon natural almond extract

½ teaspoon rosewater
250 ml (9 fl oz/1 cup) cold milk

Line a strainer with a double layer of muslin (cheesecloth). Place the strainer over a bowl. Put the almonds and sugar in a blender with 250 ml (9 fl oz/1 cup) water. Blend until the almonds are well pulverized, then pour into the strainer.

Add 3 tablespoons water to the blender and blend briefly to clean the blender of any almond residue. Pour into the strainer. Press the almonds to extract as much moisture as possible, then gather up the muslin, twist the end to seal it and squeeze firmly

over the bowl, taking care that the almonds are safely enclosed. Place the muslin and almonds in the strainer again, add another 3 tablespoons water, then stir and squeeze the almonds again. Discard the almonds.

Stir in the almond extract, rosewater and milk, then taste and add a little more sugar if necessary. Chill before serving. (If you can find them, float an unsprayed fragrant pink rose petal or two on top of each drink.)

SERVES 4

Hand-power is required to extract the almond milk from its muslin 'bag'. Wash hands well before making this delicious, fragrant drink.

Beghrir

Semolina Pancakes

The resemblance to English crumpets is apparent, but once they are tasted, there is no comparison. These light-as-air pancakes are made with flour and very fine semolina, resulting in pancakes that beg for lashings of butter and honey.

4 teaspoons active dried yeast
250 g (9 oz/2 cups) plain (all-purpose) flour
250 g (9 oz/1²/₃ cups) very fine semolina
½ teaspoon salt
2 eggs

125 ml (4 fl oz/½ cup) lukewarm milk
vegetable oil, for coating
unsalted butter, to serve
warm honey, to serve

Dissolve the dried yeast in 125 ml (4 fl oz/½ cup) of lukewarm water, then stir in 3 teaspoons of the flour. Cover with a cloth and leave in a warm place for 15 minutes, or until frothy.

Sift the remaining flour, semolina and salt into a mixing bowl and make a well in the centre. Beat the eggs lightly with the lukewarm milk and pour into the flour mixture, then add the yeast mixture and 375 ml (13 fl oz/1½ cups) lukewarm water. Starting with the flour surrounding the well and working outwards, bring the flour into the liquid, beating well with a balloon whisk for 5–7 minutes until smooth. The batter should have the consistency of thick cream. Cover the bowl with a folded tea towel (dish towel) and leave in a warm place for 1 hour, or until doubled in bulk and frothy.

Fill a saucepan one-third full with water, bring to a simmer, then place a large heatproof plate over the top. Place a tea towel (dish towel), folded in quarters, on the plate.

Heat a heavy cast-iron frying pan or crepe pan over high heat. Reduce the heat to medium and rub the pan with a wad of paper towel dipped in oil. Pour in a small ladleful (about 3 tablespoons) of batter and, using the bottom of the ladle, quickly shape into a round about 15 cm (6 in) in diameter. Work quickly and try to make the top as even as possible. Cook until the top of the pancake looks dry and is peppered with holes from the bubbles. While it is not traditional, you can turn it over and briefly brown the bubbly side.

Remove the pancake to the folds of the tea towel, and cover to keep warm. Overlap the pancakes rather than stack them. Repeat with the remaining batter, oiling the pan with the wad of paper towel between each pancake. Serve hot with butter and warm honey.

PICTURE ON PAGE 204   MAKES 16

Semolina Pancakes
(recipe on page 203)

KERMOUS MA'EL WARD B'LOUZ WA'ASSEL

Figs with Rosewater, Almonds and Honey

Fresh figs are one of the delights of late summer and autumn. While perfect on their own, they are sometimes prepared in this way and look very attractive served at the end of a banquet, with their pink flower interior exposed.

12 fresh purple-skinned figs
50 g (2 oz/⅓ cup) blanched almonds, lightly toasted

3–4 teaspoons rosewater
1–2 tablespoons honey

Wash the figs gently and pat them dry with paper towel. Starting from the stem end, cut each of the figs into quarters, almost to the base, then gently open out and put on a serving platter. Cover and chill in the refrigerator for 1 hour, or until needed.

Roughly chop the toasted almonds and set aside. Drizzle about ¼ teaspoon of the rosewater onto the exposed centre of each of the figs, and sprinkle the chopped almonds over the top. Drizzle a little honey over the nuts and serve immediately.

PICTURE ON OPPOSITE PAGE

SERVES 2

'ASSEER DALAAH BIL MA'EL WARD

Watermelon Juice with Rosewater

Watermelon juice is a summertime favourite, and not only in Morocco. The addition of rosewater turns a pleasant drink into a divine one on a hot day. Wipe the watermelon skin with a damp cloth before removing the succulent pink flesh.

1.5 kg (3 lb 5 oz) watermelon

1 teaspoon rosewater

Chill the watermelon thoroughly. Remove the rind and cut the pink flesh into thick chunks that will fit into the juice extractor feed tube. Extract the watermelon juice into a pitcher. Take care when extracting the juice, as the seeds have a tendency to jump out of the feed tube.

Add the rosewater and pour into two tall glasses, or store the juice in the refrigerator until ready to serve.

SERVES 2–3

M'HANNCHA

Almond Filo Coil

M'hanncha, meaning 'snake', is an almond paste-filled pastry made with Morocco's warkha pastry (filo pastry is a good substitute). The pastry is served at celebrations, with guests breaking off pieces from the coil. Serve with mint tea or coffee.

1 small egg, separated
200 g (7 oz/2 cups) ground almonds
30 g (1 oz/⅓ cup) flaked almonds
125 g (5 oz/1 cup) icing (confectioners') sugar
1 teaspoon finely grated lemon zest
¼ teaspoon natural almond extract

1 tablespoon rosewater
90 g (3 oz) unsalted butter or smen (page 243)
9 sheets filo pastry
pinch of ground cinnamon
icing (confectioners') sugar, extra, to serve

Preheat the oven to 180°C (350°F/Gas 4). Lightly grease a 20 cm (8 in) round spring-form tin.

Put the egg white in a bowl and beat lightly with a fork. Add the ground almonds and flaked almonds, the icing sugar, lemon zest, almond extract and rosewater. Mix to a paste.

Divide the mixture into four and roll each portion on a cutting board into a sausage shape about 5 cm (2 in) shorter than the length of filo pastry – about 42 cm (16½ in) long and 1 cm (½ in) thick. If the paste is too sticky to roll, dust the cutting board with icing sugar.

Melt the butter in a small saucepan, then keep it warm by placing the saucepan in another pan filled with hot water.

Remove one sheet of filo pastry and place the rest in the folds of a dry tea towel (dish towel) or cover them with plastic wrap to prevent them drying out. Brush the filo sheet with melted butter, then cover with another sheet of filo, brushing the top with butter. Ease one of the almond rolls off the board and onto the buttered pastry, laying it along the length of the pastry, 2.5 cm (1 in) in from the base and sides. Roll up to enclose the filling. Form into a coil and sit the coil, seam-side down, in the centre of the tin, tucking under the unfilled ends to enclose the filling. Continue in this manner to make three more pastry coils, shaping each around the smaller coil to make one large coil. If the coil breaks, cut small pieces of the remaining filo sheet, brush with a little egg yolk and press the filo onto the breaks.

Add the cinnamon to the remaining egg yolk and brush all over the coil. Bake for 30–35 minutes, or until golden brown. Dust with the extra icing sugar if desired and serve warm. This sweet pastry can be stored at room temperature for up to 2 days.

SERVES 8

GHORIBA

Semolina Biscuits

Ghoriba are baked from the Middle East to Morocco. Ingredients vary a little; this Moroccan version uses very fine semolina as well as flour, but you can replace it with plain flour if the required semolina is unavailable (see glossary).

250 g (9 oz) unsalted butter
150 g (5½ oz/1¼ cups) plain (all-purpose) flour
125 g (4½ oz/1 cup) icing (confectioners') sugar
250 g (9 oz/2 cups) very fine semolina

2 eggs, beaten
1 teaspoon natural vanilla extract
1 egg white, lightly beaten
30 g (1 oz/¼ cup) split, blanched almonds

Melt the butter in a heavy-based saucepan over low heat. Skim off and discard the froth, then pour the clarified butter into a mixing bowl, leaving the white milk solids in the pan. Set aside until cool.

Sift the flour and icing sugar into a bowl, add the semolina and a pinch of salt and mix thoroughly. When the butter is cool but still liquid, stir in the eggs and the vanilla, then add the dry ingredients, mixing to a firm dough. Knead well, then cover the bowl with plastic wrap and leave for 1 hour.

Line two baking trays with baking paper. Preheat the oven to 180°C (350°F/Gas 4).

Knead the dough again until smooth and pliant. Take 3 level teaspoons of dough and shape into a smooth ball, then shape the remaining dough into balls of the same size. Place on the prepared trays 2.5 cm (1 in) apart, as these do not spread. Brush the tops lightly with the egg white and press an almond on top of each biscuit, which will also help to flatten the biscuits a little. Bake for 20 minutes, or until lightly golden in colour. Cool on the trays. When cold, store in an airtight container.

MAKES ABOUT 48

To clarify butter, melt it in a pan. When the frothing subsides, the milk solids sink to the bottom. Skim and pour the clear oil into a bowl, leaving the milk solids in the pan.

SEFFA

Sweet Couscous

Couscous is served as the final savoury dish of a banquet and interestingly a sweet couscous is often served. As it is a popular dish at palace banquets, the more expensive nuts – pistachios and pine nuts – are often used along with the traditional almonds.

80 g (3 oz/½ cup) combined pistachio nuts, pine nuts
    and blanched almonds
40 g (1½ oz/¼ cup) dried apricots
250 g (9 oz/1⅓ cups) instant couscous
55 g (2 oz/¼ cup) caster (superfine) sugar

90 g (3 oz) unsalted butter, softened
½ teaspoon ground cinnamon
2 tablespoons caster (superfine) sugar, extra
375 ml (13 fl oz/1½ cups) hot milk

Preheat the oven to 160°C (315°F/Gas 2–3). Spread the nuts on a baking tray and bake for about 5 minutes, or until lightly golden. Allow to cool, then roughly chop and place in a bowl. Slice the apricots into matchstick-sized pieces. Add to the nuts and toss to combine.

Put the couscous and sugar in a large bowl and cover with 250 ml (9 fl oz/1 cup) boiling water. Stir well, then add the butter and a pinch of salt.

Stir until the butter melts. Cover with a tea towel (dish towel) and set aside for 10 minutes. Fluff the grains with a fork, then toss through half the fruit and nut mixture.

To serve, pile the warm couscous in the centre of a platter. Arrange the remaining nut mixture around the edge. Combine the cinnamon and extra sugar in a small bowl for sprinkling. Pass around the hot milk in a pitcher for guests to help themselves.

SERVES 4–6

DALAAH BIL MA'EL WARD WAL NA'NA'

Watermelon with Rosewater and Mint

2 kg (4 lb 8 oz) wedge of watermelon
3 teaspoons rosewater

small, fresh mint leaves, to serve

Working over a plate to catch any juice, remove the skin and the rind from the watermelon and cut the flesh into 2.5 cm (1 in) cubes, removing any visible seeds. Pile the cubes in a bowl.

Pour the watermelon juice into a small pitcher and stir in the rosewater. Sprinkle over the watermelon, cover and chill for 1 hour, or until ready to serve. Scatter with the mint leaves and serve chilled.

SERVES 4–6

ATAY BIL NA'NA'
Mint Tea

1 bunch fresh spearmint
2 teaspoons Chinese gunpowder green tea

2 tablespoons white sugar, or to taste

Cut the ends off the mint stalks, leaving the leafy sprigs. Wash well, then shake dry and roll in a tea towel (dish towel) to absorb the excess moisture. Alternatively, dry the mint in a salad spinner.

Rinse a 1 litre (36 fl oz/4 cup) teapot with boiling water, add the tea and a little boiling water, swirl briefly, let it settle, then carefully pour out the water to remove any tea dust. Half-fill the pot with boiling water. Take a handful of the mint sprigs, crush lightly in the hand and add to the pot. Add more crushed mint sprigs until the pot is three-quarters full. Add the sugar and fill the pot with boiling water. Let the tea brew for 3 minutes.

Pour out a glass of tea and pour back into the pot. Repeat, twice more to mix the tea and to dissolve the sugar. Serve the tea in tea glasses, pouring it from a height to aerate the tea. Add an uncrushed mint sprig to each glass.

SERVES 4–6

GHORIBA B'LOOZ
Almond Macaroons

300 g (10½ oz/3 cups) ground almonds
150 g (5½ oz/1¼ cups) icing (confectioners') sugar
1½ teaspoons baking powder
½ teaspoon ground cinnamon

1 egg
2 teaspoons grated lemon zest
1 tablespoon rosewater
3 tablespoons icing (confectioners') sugar, extra

Put the ground almonds in a mixing bowl and sift in the icing sugar, baking powder and cinnamon. Stir until well combined. Beat the egg with the lemon zest and rosewater and then add to the dry ingredients. Mix to a firm paste and knead lightly.

Line two baking trays with baking paper. Sift the extra icing sugar into a shallow dish. Preheat the oven to 180°C (350°F/Gas 4).

Break off pieces of dough the size of walnuts and roll into balls, oiling your hands lightly to prevent the dough sticking. Press into the icing sugar and flatten slightly. Lift carefully so that the topping is not disturbed, and place on the trays, sugar-side up, spacing them 5 cm (2 in) apart to allow for spreading. Bake for 20 minutes. Leave on the trays for 10 minutes before removing to a wire rack to cool. Store in an airtight container.

MAKES ABOUT 36

TEA CEREMONY

Most of the herbs in Morocco are native to the Mediterranean region and the Middle East. Herbal infusions have always been popular in Morocco. Mint grows there particularly well, with mint tea taken for indigestion and as a calmative.

During the Crimean War in 1854, embargoes prevented British tea merchants selling to their usual customers and they looked elsewhere for new markets. Two of these were Tangier and Mogador. The Moroccans embraced tea drinking with enthusiasm, and soon found that the pale greenish brew complemented their favoured mint infusion. The preferred tea is Chinese gunpowder green tea. The teapot (barrad) is similar to that of the British 'Manchester' in shape, with a bulbous body, a domed lid and a long spout that is ideal for pouring the tea from a height with accuracy. It is made in silver plate, aluminium or stainless steel.

Besides mint, ingredients such as lemon verbena, saffron, orange blossoms or cinnamon are used in some areas for additional flavour. The type of mint used is very important. In Morocco they use a variety of spearmint that is known as Moroccan mint, *Mentha crispa*. Its leaves are not as slender as spearmint, *M. spicata*, and are more crinkled and a deeper green in colour. However spearmint is just as acceptable. Just as important is the tea used; Chinese gunpowder green tea is the preferred tea. Each tea leaf is rolled into a compact, round pellet. An alternative is Hyson; again individual small tea leaves are rolled up and twisted. When the tea is brewing, the tea leaves open up like tiny flower petals, so there is no need to strain it. The mint in the pot does a good job of that anyway.

The tea ceremony is carried out at home after entertaining dinner guests. Equipment is set out on a low, round table – a silver three-legged tray holding patterned tea glasses, a silver teapot, a brass hammer for breaking lumps from the sugar cone, and silver boxes for tea, mint and sugar lumps. With the boiling water from a *samovar*, the tea is poured into each glass from a height to aerate it. Etiquette decrees that each guest has three glasses. And how do you drink tea from a glass? Grip its rim with the thumb and forefinger of the right hand and sip, sip, sip …

Mint tea is served in cafés, poured from a height to create a froth; other purveyors of the brew also provide mint tea to shop owners for their own refreshment, or to seal a deal with a customer. Young men carrying trays with glasses of mint tea are a common sight in the souks, as nearby stallholders also take advantage of this service.

Kaab el Ghzal

Gazelles' Horns

The most popular pastries in Morocco, sold at street stalls and in patisseries, and, on festive occasions, made in enormous quantities by groups of women. The pastry shrinks around the filling during baking, allowing the filling to dominate.

PASTRY
300 g (10½ oz/2½ cups) plain (all-purpose) flour
1 egg yolk
30 g (1 oz) butter, melted
2 tablespoons orange flower water

ALMOND FILLING
300 g (10½ oz/3 cups) ground almonds
90 g (3 oz/¾ cup) icing (confectioners') sugar, plus extra to dust
1 tablespoon orange flower water
1 egg white, lightly beaten
30 g (1 oz) unsalted butter, melted
½ teaspoon ground cinnamon
¼ teaspoon natural almond extract

To make the pastry, sift the flour into a mixing bowl and make a well in the centre. Beat the egg yolk into 125 ml (4 fl oz/½ cup) water and pour it into the flour with the butter and orange flower water. Mix to a soft dough, then knead in the bowl for 5 minutes to form a smooth, elastic dough. Divide into two pieces, wrap in plastic wrap and rest for 20 minutes.

To make the almond filling, mix all of the filling ingredients to a stiff paste. Shape 3 level teaspoons of filling into a ball. Shape the remaining filling into balls of the same size. Roll each ball between your palms into logs 7.5 cm (3 in) long, tapering at each end. Place on baking paper and set aside. Preheat the oven to 180°C (350°F/Gas 4).

Thinly roll out one ball of the prepared dough on a lightly floured work surface, to a rectangle about 30 x 40 cm (12 x 16 in), with the short side towards you. Place three almond shapes 5 cm (2 in) from the edge of the pastry closest to you, 2.5 cm (1 in) apart and half that from each end. Lightly brush the pastry along the edge and between the almond shapes with cold water. Lift and stretch the end of the pastry over the filling and press firmly around the filling to seal. Cut around the filling with a fluted pastry wheel, leaving a 1 cm (½ in) border around the filling. As each pastry is placed on the baking tray, bend it upwards on the filling side into a crescent. Using a cocktail pick, prick the tops of the pastries four times. Straighten the edge of the pastry with a knife and repeat until all the filling and pastry is used, including the trimmings.

Bake the pastries for 12–15 minutes, or until cooked but still pale. Transfer to a wire rack and dust with sifted icing sugar while hot. Store in an airtight container when cool.

MAKES ABOUT 28

Mulhalabya

Almond Cream Pudding

This creamy milk pudding is Middle Eastern in origin, thickened with cornflour, ground rice and ground almonds. Rosewater gives it a subtle fragrance. Top it with toasted slivered almonds and a sprinkling of pomegranate seeds when in season.

500 ml (17 fl oz/2 cups) milk
3 tablespoons caster (superfine) sugar
2 tablespoons cornflour (cornstarch)
1 tablespoon ground rice
70 g (2 oz/⅔ cup) ground almonds

1 teaspoon rosewater
2 tablespoons slivered (or flaked) almonds, toasted
1 teaspoon caster (superfine) sugar, extra
½ teaspoon ground cinnamon

Put the milk and sugar in a heavy-based saucepan and heat over medium heat until the sugar has dissolved. Bring to the boil.

Meanwhile, in a large heatproof bowl, combine the cornflour and ground rice with 3 tablespoons water and mix to a smooth paste. Add the boiling milk, stirring constantly with a balloon whisk, then return to the same saucepan. Stir over medium heat until thickened and bubbling, then add the ground almonds and simmer over low heat for 5 minutes, stirring occasionally until thick and creamy. Add the rosewater and then remove from the heat. Stir occasionally to cool a little, then spoon into glasses or serving bowls. Refrigerate for 1 hour.

Mix the toasted slivered almonds with the extra sugar and the cinnamon and sprinkle over the top of the pudding before serving.

SERVES 4

Stir the ground almonds into the bubbling milk mixture, then reduce the heat and simmer until thick and creamy.

KENEFFA

Crisp Pastries with Almond Cream

Fried warkha pastry is used for this traditional dessert assembled in a tall stack with almond cream and almonds. It collapses when portions are broken off with the fingers but making individual pastry stacks with won ton wrappers solves this problem.

ALMOND CREAM
750 ml (26 fl oz/3 cups) milk
35 g (1¼ oz/¼ cup) cornflour (cornstarch)
60 g (2¼ oz/¼ cup) caster (superfine) sugar
50 g (1¾ oz/½ cup) ground almonds
¼ teaspoon natural almond extract
1½ tablespoons rosewater

100 g (3½ oz/⅔ cup) blanched almonds, lightly toasted
2 tablespoons icing (confectioners') sugar, sifted,
   plus extra, to serve
½ teaspoon ground cinnamon
36 square won ton wrappers, at room temperature
vegetable oil, for frying
unsprayed rose petals, to serve

To make the almond cream, put 125 ml (4 fl oz/ ½ cup) of the milk in a large heatproof bowl, add the cornflour and mix to a thin paste. Bring the remaining milk to the boil until it froths up. Mix the cornflour paste again, then pour in the boiling milk, mixing constantly with a balloon whisk. Pour this back into the saucepan and stir in the sugar and ground almonds. Return to the heat and stir constantly with a wooden spoon until thickened and bubbling. Pour back into the bowl and stir in the almond extract and rosewater. Press a piece of plastic wrap on the surface and leave to cool. Just before using the cream, stir briskly with a balloon whisk to smooth it; if it is too thick, stir in a little milk to give a pouring consistency.

Roughly chop the toasted almonds, mix with the icing sugar and cinnamon, and set aside. Lightly brush a won ton wrapper with water and press another firmly on top. Repeat with the remaining wrappers until there are 18 pairs.

In a large, deep frying pan, add oil to a depth of 1 cm (½ in) and place over high heat. When the oil is hot, but not smoking, reduce the heat to medium and add two pairs of won ton wrappers. Fry for about 20 seconds until lightly browned, turning to brown evenly. Remove the pastries with tongs and drain on paper towel. Repeat with the remaining squares.

To assemble the pastries, put a fried pastry square in the centre of each plate. Drizzle with a little almond cream and sprinkle with a heaped teaspoon of the almond mixture. Top with another pastry square, cream and almonds. Finish with another pastry square. Scatter with unsprayed rose petals, sift a little icing sugar over the top and serve with the remaining almond cream in a pitcher.

SERVES 6

'Asseer Dle Zhib wa Ma'el Ward

Grape Juice with Rosewater

Black grapes give a pleasing colour to this delicious drink. Fortunately many seedless grape varieties are available. Green grapes may also be used for a pleasant but lighter flavoured beverage – omit the cinnamon.

500 g (1 lb 2 oz) chilled seedless black grapes
1 teaspoon rosewater

ground cinnamon, to serve (optional)

Wash the grapes very well and pull from the stems. Drain well and feed the grapes into juice extractor, catching the juice in a pitcher. When the grapes are juiced, let the juice settle and skim off any dark froth. Cover the pitcher with plastic wrap and chill for at least 1 hour.

Decant the juice into two tall glasses, leaving any sediment in the pitcher. Stir ½ teaspoon rosewater into each glass and dust the top lightly with ground cinnamon, if desired.

PICTURE ON OPPOSITE PAGE

SERVES 2

Sfargel Helwa bil Ma'el Ward

Quinces in Rosewater Syrup

Quinces require lengthy cooking to take on an attractive rosy hue. Leaving the skin and core on shortens the process; it is easy to pull off the skin once cooked. Rosewater is a good flavouring for quinces, its floral tones enhancing their flavour.

2 quinces, washed well and quartered
175 g (6 oz/¾ cup) caster (superfine) sugar

thinly peeled zest of ½ lemon
2–3 teaspoons rosewater

Place the quinces in a saucepan and cover with water. Bring to the boil, then cover and simmer over low heat for 40 minutes, or until the quinces are almost tender and are beginning to colour. Drain in a fine sieve over a bowl and return the liquid to the saucepan.

Add the sugar and lemon zest to the pan and stir over heat until the sugar dissolves, then leave to

simmer gently without stirring while you prepare the quince. Pull the skin from the quince quarters, remove the cores and halve each quarter. Place the quince slices in the syrup with rosewater to taste and simmer, uncovered, for a further 30 minutes, or until the quinces are tender and have a rosy hue. Remove the lemon zest and serve warm or chilled.

SERVES 4–6

Tamra bil Gooz
Date and Nut Candies

The Berbers, especially the nomadic tribes, relied on the date as a staple foodstuff. They made dates into sweetmeats with a range of other ingredients. The inclusion of smen and nuts increases the energy value of this particular sweetmeat.

150 g (5½ oz/1½ cups) walnut halves or
  155 g (5¾ oz/1 cup) blanched almonds
2 tablespoons sesame seeds

100 g (3½ oz) smen (page 243), or ghee
600 g (1 lb 5 oz/3⅓ cups) pitted dried dates,
  roughly chopped

Preheat the oven to 180°C (350°F/Gas 4). Line an 18 cm (7 in) square baking tin with baking paper, ensuring the paper overhangs the opposite ends of the tin. Spread the walnuts or almonds on a baking tray and bake for 5 minutes, or until lightly toasted. Chop roughly. Bake the sesame seeds on a baking tray for a few minutes until golden.

Melt the smen in a large heavy-based saucepan. Add the dates and cook, covered, over low heat for 10 minutes, stirring often, until the dates soften. Remove from the heat. Using the back of a spoon

dipped in cold water, spread half the dates over the base of the prepared tin. Scatter the nuts on top and press into the dates. Spread the remaining date mixture over the nuts and smooth the surface with wet fingers, pressing down firmly. Sprinkle the dates with the sesame seeds and press lightly. Set aside until cool.

Remove the set mixture from the tin using the overhanging baking paper as handles. Cut into small diamonds to serve.

SERVES 6–8

Use the back of a spoon dipped in cold water to spread the dates over the base of the tin.

Briouat bil Fakiya
Dried Fruit Pastries

For these pastries, use the softer dessert figs if possible. The pastries will keep in a sealed container for 2–3 days if necessary. If the weather is humid, wait until just before serving to sift the icing sugar on top.

125 g (5 oz) smen (page 243), melted
165 g (5¾ oz/1 cup) blanched almonds
80 g (2¾ oz/½ cup) chopped dessert figs
   (soft, dried figs)
80 g (2¾ oz/½ cup) pitted, chopped dates

1 tablespoon orange flower water
12 sheets filo pastry
icing (confectioners') sugar, to serve

In a small frying pan, warm 1 tablespoon of the melted smen, add the blanched almonds and cook over medium heat, stirring often, until golden. Tip immediately into the food processor bowl, along with any smen from the pan. Cool, then process until the almonds are finely chopped. Add the figs, dates and orange flower water and process to a thick paste, scraping down the side of the bowl as necessary. Turn out onto the work surface, rub your hands with a little of the melted smen and gather the paste into a ball. Roll into a 23 cm (9 in) log and cut it into 18 pieces. Roll each piece into a 10 cm (4 in) log and set aside on baking paper.

Stack the pastry on a cutting surface with the long side in front of you. Mark the pastry in three equal strips and cut through the stack with a sharp knife to make strips 12.5–14 cm (4½–5½ in) wide and 28–30 cm (11¼–12 in) long. Stack the strips in the folds of a dry tea towel (dish towel). (Use extra sheets if the filo is less than 38 cm (15 in) long.)

Place a strip of pastry with the narrow end nearest you and brush with the warm, melted smen. Top with another strip and brush the top with smen. Place the shaped filling 1.5 cm (⅝ in) in from the base and sides of the strip. Fold the end of the filo over the filling, fold in the sides and brush the side folds with more smen. Roll to the end and place seam-side down on a greased baking tray. Repeat with the remaining ingredients.

Preheat the oven to 180°C (350°F/Gas 4); do this after the rolls are completed so the kitchen remains cool while shaping. Lightly brush the tops of the rolls with smen and bake for 20 minutes, or until lightly golden. Sift icing sugar over the rolls while hot. Store when cool in a sealed container.

MAKES 18

SFENJ

Doughnuts

All over Morocco you will find doughnut makers, with cauldrons of hot oil, frying doughnuts to order. These are strung on lengths of palm frond and tied, to be taken home or to a café and eaten plain with very sweet mint tea. Dip in sugar if desired.

2 teaspoons active dried yeast
½ teaspoon caster (superfine) sugar
375 g (13 oz/3 cups) plain (all-purpose) flour

vegetable oil, for deep-frying
caster (superfine) sugar, to serve (optional)
ground cinnamon, to serve (optional)

Dissolve the dried yeast in 125 ml (4 fl oz/½ cup) lukewarm water and stir in the sugar. Mix the flour and ½ teaspoon salt in a mixing bowl and make a well in the centre. Pour in the yeast mixture and an extra 125 ml (4 fl oz/½ cup) lukewarm water. Stir sufficient flour into the liquid to form a thin batter. Leave for 15 minutes until bubbles form. Gradually stir in the remaining flour, then mix with your hand to form a soft dough. If too stiff, add a little more water. Knead for 5 minutes in the bowl until the dough is smooth and elastic. Pour a little oil down the side of the bowl, turn the ball of dough to coat with oil, cover with a cloth and leave for 1 hour, or until doubled in bulk.

Punch down the dough, turn it out onto a work surface and divide it into 20 even portions. Lightly oil your hands and two baking trays. Roll each portion of dough into a smooth ball and place on one of the trays. Using your index finger, poke a hole in the centre of each ball while on the tray,

then twirl it around your finger until the hole enlarges to 2 cm (¾ in) in diameter. Repeat with the remaining balls of dough.

Fill a large saucepan one-third full of oil and heat to 190°C (375°F) or until a cube of bread dropped in the oil browns in 10 seconds. Have a long metal skewer on hand and begin with the doughnut first shaped. Carefully drop the doughnut into the oil, immediately put the skewer in the centre and twirl it around in a circular motion for 2–3 seconds to keep the hole open. Fry for 1½–2 minutes, turning to brown evenly. Once this process is mastered, drop 2–3 doughnuts at a time into the oil, briefly twirling the skewer in the centre of the first before adding the next. When cooked, lift out with the skewer onto a tray lined with paper towel.

Eat while hot with mint tea or sweet coffee. While it is not traditional, you can toss the doughnuts in caster sugar, adding ground cinnamon if desired.

MAKES 20

Rozz bil Hleeb

Rice Pudding

This is served in a communal dish in Moroccan households, and eaten with a spoon. The topping can vary – usually dabs of butter are placed on the warm pudding, but chopped toasted almonds, or raisins and honey as in the recipe, can also be used.

110 g (4 oz/½ cup) short-grain rice
1125 ml (39 fl oz/4½ cups) milk
2 tablespoons raisins
2 tablespoons orange flower water
55 g (2 oz/¼ cup) caster (superfine) sugar

55 g (2 oz/½ cup) ground almonds
2 tablespoons cornflour (cornstarch)
¼ teaspoon natural almond extract
2 tablespoons honey

Put the rice in a large heavy-based saucepan with 250 ml (9 fl oz/1 cup) water and a pinch of salt. Cook over medium heat, stirring occasionally, for 5 minutes, or until the water has been absorbed.

Set aside 125 ml (4 fl oz/½ cup) of the milk. Stir 250 ml (9 fl oz/1 cup) of the remaining milk into the rice, bring to a simmer, and when the rice has absorbed the milk, add another 250 ml (9 fl oz/ 1 cup) milk. Continue to add the remaining milk in this manner, ensuring each addition of milk is absorbed before adding the next. The rice should be very soft in 30 minutes, with the final addition of milk barely absorbed.

Meanwhile, steep the raisins in 2 teaspoons of the orange flower water for 15 minutes.

Mix the sugar with the ground almonds to break up any lumps in the almonds. Stir into the rice mixture and simmer gently for 2–3 minutes. Mix the cornflour with the reserved milk until smooth and stir into the rice. When thickened, simmer for 2 minutes. Remove the pan from the heat and stir in the almond extract and the remaining orange flower water. Stir the pudding occasionally to cool it a little.

Pour the pudding into a serving bowl and when a slight skin forms on the top, sprinkle with the soaked raisins and drizzle with honey. Cool completely before serving in individual bowls.

SERVES 8

As ready-prepared ground almonds can be lumpy, mix with the sugar to break up lumps.

Food Journey

PASTRY SHOP

∞∞∞∞∞∞∞∞∞∞∞∞∞∞∞∞∞∞∞∞∞

The popularity of Moroccan and French pastries is confirmed with the number of pastry shops, open-fronted, decorative stalls, or merely a vendor guarding his glass cabinet stacked with his specialities. One constant is that you are seldom disappointed with your choices.

Moroccan pastries have links to those of the Middle East, but are completely different in their final form. Ghoriba are found from the Middle East to Morocco in various forms, but Moroccans make baklawa-type pastries their own way – unique and just as delicious. The similarities are in the ingredients used – almonds, cinnamon, orange flower water, rosewater, a hint of lemon zest, honey – these are the popular ingredients for making many of these sweet delicacies. Walnuts, dates, raisins, dried figs, caraway and sesame seeds are also used according to the art of the pâtissière.

While filo pastry is used in the recipes in this book, warkha is the only pastry used in Morocco. Its pedigree is Persian, and it was perfected in the palace kitchens. Delicate and tissue thin, it is made by a process that is now left to experts. A sticky, unleavened dough is prepared, rested and divided into small balls. The warkha maker inverts a tobsil, a round, tinned copper pan, over a charcoal brazier in which the heat has been carefully controlled with ash. When heated, the tobsil is rubbed with an oily cloth. A ball of dough is rapidly tapped repeatedly onto the heated tobsil. This continues in a rhythmic way until the dabs of dough join to form a complete sheet. When it is dry around the edges, each sheet is peeled off and placed in a stack. The process is so rapid that a sheet is usually made in a matter of seconds. The first two or three often fail, but after that, perfect sheets are peeled off every time, provided that the tobsil is oiled between making each sheet.

An Aladdin's 'cave' of Moroccan and French cookies and pastries awaits the shoppers who wish to buy a treat to enjoy with their mint tea. They may choose briouats with various fillings, shaped into triangles, rolls or coils to be fried and dipped in syrup, or baked to perfection. Or perhaps some meringues, sweet rusks, almond filo coils or gazelles' horns.

KERMOUS HELWA
Figs in Syrup

Dried figs are a popular snack food as they are, but in winter they are soaked and cooked with typical Moroccan spices, turning them into a fruit compote. While not traditional, yoghurt can be served with them.

375 g (13 oz) dried figs
blanched almonds, one per fig
3 whole cloves
3 bruised cardamom pods
½ teaspoon black peppercorns

115 g (4 oz/½ cup) caster (superfine) sugar
thinly peeled zest of ½ lemon
1 cinnamon stick
thick yoghurt, to serve

Rinse the figs and place in a bowl with cold water to cover generously. Soak for 8 hours, or until plump. Drain the soaking water into a saucepan.

Insert an almond into each fig from the base. Tie the cloves, cardamom pods and peppercorns in a piece of muslin (cheesecloth).

Place the saucepan with the soaking liquid over medium–high heat. Add the sugar, stirring until dissolved. Bring to the boil, then add the spices, lemon zest, cinnamon stick and figs. Return to the boil, then simmer for 30 minutes, or until tender. Transfer the figs to a dish and strain the syrup over them. Serve warm or chilled with yoghurt.

SERVES 4–6

AMALOU
Almond and Honey Spread

100 g (3½ oz/1 cup) ground almonds
2 tablespoons argan, walnut or macadamia nut oil

1 tablespoon dark honey
3–4 drops natural almond extract

In a bowl, mix the ground almonds with a pinch of salt and the nut oil. Stir well and mix in the honey and the almond extract. The amalou should have a soft, spreading consistency; if necessary add a little more oil and honey. The amount of oil depends on the moistness of the ground almonds.

Serve spread on bread, beghrir (semolina pancakes, page 203) or other pancakes with additional honey if desired. The amalou can be stored in a sealed jar in the refrigerator for 3–4 weeks; bring to room temperature for serving.

MAKES 140 G (5 OZ/½ CUP)

'ASSEER DEL LITCHINE BIL MA'ZHAAR
Orange Juice with Orange Flower Water

At street stalls, perfectly stacked rows or pyramids of glowing oranges announce the orange-juice sellers. Usually it is freshly squeezed, but ask that water not be added for the ultimate taste, highlighted even more with a dash of orange flower water.

6 sweet oranges, chilled
caster (superfine) sugar, to taste

1½ teaspoons orange flower water
ground cinnamon, to serve (optional)

Using a citrus juicer, juice the oranges, then pour the juice through a sieve into a pitcher.

Stir in the caster sugar, to taste (you may not need to add any sugar if the oranges are very sweet).

Add the orange flower water. Pour into two tall glasses and lightly dust the top with cinnamon, if desired. Serve immediately.

SERVES 2

HLEEB B'LAVUKA
Avocado Milk Drink

Avocados are mainly used for this delightful drink, made in street cafés and laiteries using a blender. With blenders appearing in home kitchens, especially in the cities, this delicious drink is often enjoyed at home. Orange flower water adds an exotic flavour.

1 ripe avocado, about 225 g (8 oz), chilled
1½ tablespoons caster (superfine) sugar, or to taste

375 ml (13 fl oz/1½ cups) chilled milk
½ teaspoon orange flower water

Halve the avocado, remove the seed and, using a spoon, scoop the flesh into a blender jar. Add sugar and chilled milk. Blend until smooth and frothy.

Taste and add more sugar if necessary. Add orange flower water, blend briefly and pour into two tall glasses. Serve immediately.

SERVES 2

BASICS

An important step in mastering any cuisine is learning the basic recipes and techniques. Straight from the recipe journal, here are the ones no Moroccan cook would be without.

Harissa
Hot Chilli Paste

Harissa is extremely hot, so use it with caution. For a milder version of this fiery paste, slit the chillies (instead of chopping them) before soaking in the boiling water, then scrape out the seeds before processing as per the recipe.

125 g (5 oz) dried red chillies, stems removed
1 tablespoon dried mint
1 tablespoon ground coriander
1 tablespoon ground cumin

1 teaspoon ground caraway seeds
10 garlic cloves, chopped
125 ml (4 fl oz/½ cup) olive oil

To prepare a storage jar, preheat the oven to 120°C (235°F/Gas ½). Wash the jar and lid in hot soapy water and rinse with hot water. Put the jar in the oven for 20 minutes, or until fully dry. Do not dry with a tea towel (dish towel).

Roughly chop the chillies, then cover with boiling water and soak for 1 hour. Drain the chillies, put them in a food processor and add the mint, spices, garlic, 1 tablespoon of the oil and ½ teaspoon salt.

Process for 20 seconds, then scrape down the side of the bowl and process for another 30 seconds. With the motor running, gradually add the rest of the olive oil. Scrape down the side of the bowl when necessary.

Spoon the chilli paste into the clean storage jar, cover with a thin layer of olive oil and seal. Label and date. Harissa will keep in the refrigerator for up to 6 months.

FILLS A 600 ML (21 FL OZ/2½ CUP) JAR

Ras el Hanout
Spice Blend

½ teaspoon ground cloves
½ teaspoon cayenne pepper
2 teaspoons ground allspice
2 teaspoons ground cumin
2 teaspoons ground ginger
2 teaspoons ground turmeric

2 teaspoons ground black pepper
2 teaspoons ground cardamom
3 teaspoons ground cinnamon
3 teaspoons ground coriander
2 nutmegs, freshly grated
  (or 6 teaspoons ground nutmeg)

Purchase the freshest spices possible. Combine all the ground spices in a clean jar, seal and store in a cool, dark place. Alternatively, use whole spices in the same quantities and grind in a spice grinder. However, grate the nutmegs separately as most grinders cannot cope with them.

MAKES 60 G (2¼ OZ)

Smen

Clarified Butter

Butter is melted and heated for a lengthy time until the milk solids sink and begin to brown, giving a nutty flavour. For traditional clarified butter, skim the froth and pour the clear fat into a container before the milk solids brown. Ghee is a substitute.

250 g (9 oz) salted or unsalted butter, diced

Put the butter in a heavy-based saucepan over low heat. If using gas, place the pan over the smallest burner and use a heat diffuser, because butter has a tendency to spit if the heat is not low enough.

Simmer very gently for 25 minutes. Pour through a sieve lined with muslin (cheesecloth), set over a bowl. The clear oil is the smen and has a slightly nutty taste.

Store in a sealed jar in the refrigerator, although it can safely be stored at room temperature, as is done in Morocco. This keeps for many months.

For sweet pastries using filo, smen is recommended, even with its slightly nutty flavour, because if melted unclarified butter is used any milk solids brushed onto the filo become dark when cooked, spoiling the appearance of the baked pastry.

MAKES 175 G (6 OZ)

Smen bil Za'atar

Herbed Clarified Butter

Traditionally, this is stored in a stone jar and buried for a year or more, giving it a strong cheesy flavour. It is much loved stirred through couscous. A short cut is to mix together equal quantities of herbed smen and blue cheese.

2 tablespoons dried za'atar, or dried Greek thyme
2 teaspoons coarse salt

250 g (9 oz) salted or unsalted butter

Put the za'atar and salt in a sieve lined with muslin (cheesecloth). Following the directions above, heat the butter and slowly pour it through the herb and salt mixture. Store in a sealed jar in the refrigerator.

In Morocco, herbed smen is aged for months, even years, and has a strong, cheesy flavour. This is a much milder version.

MAKES 175 G (6 OZ)

KSEKSOU

Couscous (Steaming Method)

Both regular couscous and instant couscous should be prepared by steaming the grains to make them light and fluffy. The traditional method of rubbing grains to remove lumps and 'air' the grains has been replaced with a modern method.

500 g (1 lb 2 oz/2¾ cups) regular couscous (page 249)

90 g (3 oz) smen or herbed smen (page 243) or butter, diced

Put the couscous in a large, shallow bowl and cover with cold water. Stir with a balloon whisk and then pour the water off immediately through a strainer to catch any grains. Return the grains to the bowl and set aside for 10 minutes to allow the couscous to swell, stirring it occasionally with the balloon whisk to keep the grains separate.

Use the steamer section of a couscoussier, a steamer that fits snugly over a large saucepan, or a metal colander. If the steamer does not fit snugly, put a long, folded strip of foil around the rim of the pan, place steamer in position and press firmly. If the steamer has large holes, line it with a double layer of muslin (cheesecloth).

Spread the couscous in the steamer and place over the pan of food being cooked, or over a saucepan of boiling water. The base of the steamer must not touch the top of the stew or water. Cook until the steam rises through the grains, then cover and cook for a further 20 minutes. Fork through the couscous occasionally to steam it evenly.

Tip the couscous into the bowl, add the smen and ½ teaspoon salt and sprinkle with 125 ml (4 fl oz/ ½ cup) cold water. Stir again with the balloon whisk to separate the grains.

At this stage, the couscous may be covered with a damp cloth and left for several hours if necessary. About 20 minutes before the stew is ready, return the couscous to the steamer and replace over the stew or boiling water. Do not cover while steaming and fluff up occasionally with a fork. Turn into the bowl, stir well with the whisk and serve according to the recipe.

NOTE: For instant couscous, follow the directions given but only steam the couscous for 10 minutes each time.

SERVES 6–8

Rozz Za'fran

Saffron Rice

Andalusian influence is obvious in this rice dish, which is popular in northern Morocco. While Moroccans steam the rice – a lengthy process – the following uses the absorption method. A short or medium grain is the type used in Morocco.

500 g (1 lb 2 oz/2½ cups) short-grain rice
2 tablespoons olive oil

¼ teaspoon ground saffron threads
20 g (1 oz) butter

Wash the rice in a sieve until the water runs clear, then drain well.

Heat the olive oil in a heavy-based saucepan over medium heat and add the rice, stirring so that it is coated with the oil. Add 900 ml (31 fl oz/3⅔ cups) water, the saffron and ¼ teaspoon salt and stir well. Increase the heat to high. Bring to the boil and then boil for 1 minute.

Reduce the heat to low, cover the pan and cook the rice for 10–12 minutes, or until all the water has been absorbed. Steam tunnels will form holes on the surface of the rice. Turn off the heat, then leave the pan, covered, for 10 minutes. Add the butter and fluff lightly with a fork. Transfer to a serving bowl. Saffron rice is used to accompany fish dishes, but it can also be used as a substitute for couscous.

SERVES 6

Marqa del Hout

Fish Stock

1 kg (2 lb 4 oz) fish heads and bones
1 small white onion, sliced
1 carrot, sliced

4 parsley stalks
1 small leafy celery stalk, roughly chopped
6 black peppercorns

Remove the gills and any blood from the fish heads and rinse well in cold water with the bones. Place in a stock pot and add the onion, carrot, parsley and celery. Cover with 1.5 litres (52 fl oz/6 cups) water. Place over medium heat and bring slowly to simmering point, skimming as required.

Add the peppercorns and 1 teaspoon salt. Simmer for 20 minutes. Strain though a sieve lined with muslin (cheesecloth) into a bowl, then cover and refrigerate until required. Keeps for up to 4 days in the refrigerator, or freeze for up to 2 months.

MAKES 1.25 LITRES (44 FL OZ/5 CUPS)

Hamed Markad

Preserved Lemons

Make preserved lemons with ripe, new-season fruit that have not been waxed. Store-bought lemons are usually coated with a wax, which has to be removed by scrubbing in warm water with a soft-bristle brush; even then it is very difficult to remove.

8–12 thin-skinned new-season lemons
rock salt
1–2 extra lemons

black peppercorns (optional)
bay leaves (optional)

To prepare a storage jar, preheat the oven to 120°C (235°F/Gas ½). Wash the jar and lid in hot soapy water and rinse with hot water. Put the jar in the oven for 20 minutes, or until fully dry. Do not dry with a tea towel (dish towel).

If the lemons are very firm, soak them in water for 3 days, changing the water daily. Wash the lemons if soaking is not required. Cut the lemons from the stem end into quarters almost through to the base. Insert 1 tablespoon rock salt into each lemon, close it up and place in a jar. Repeat until the jar is filled, sprinkling 1 tablespoon salt between the layers. Pack the lemons into the jar as tightly as possible. Add a bay leaf and a few peppercorns to each jar if desired.

Wash the extra lemons. Add the juice of 1 lemon to each jar. Fill with slightly cooled, boiled water. Put the washed skin from a squeezed-out lemon half on top so that if any white film forms on top (which is harmless), the skin can be discarded when the jar is opened. Seal the jars and store in a cool, dark place for 4 weeks, gently shaking the jars daily for the first week to dissolve the salt. The cloudy liquid clears in this time. The lemons will keep for 6 months or more. Once the jar is opened, store in the refrigerator.

To prepare for cooking, separate a lemon into quarters and rinse under running water. Remove and discard the pulp. Rinse the rind, pat dry with paper towel and use as directed in recipes.

FILLS 1 X 2 LITRE (70 FL OZ/8 CUP) JAR OR 2 X 1 LITRE (35 FL OZ/4 CUP) JARS

GLOSSARY

ALMONDS

Whole, slivered and ground almonds are used in sweet and savoury dishes. If ground almonds (almond meal) are not available, grind slivered or whole almonds in a food processor. Use very fresh, dry almonds, and process as briefly as possible to prevent them from becoming oily; for this reason, slivered almonds are best.

ALMONDS, BLANCHED

Almonds keep better if purchased with skin on and have a better flavour when freshly blanched. To blanch, soak in boiling water for 5 minutes, then drain and slip off the skins when cool. Leave on a baking tray lined with paper towel until dry and crisp, or put in a slow oven for 5 minutes to dry thoroughly. Refrigerate in a sealed container.

ALMONDS, GREEN

These appear in souks in mid-summer, when the drupe is green and the almond shell is still soft within. They are left to soak in salted water for a day or two, then eaten whole as a snack.

ANISEED

Also known as anise seed, the pale brown seeds have a mild liquorice flavour. It is a popular flavouring and topping for bread. It is also used in sweet, rusk-like toasts called fekkas. Most households have fekkas on hand to have with their morning mint tea.

BROAD (FAVA) BEANS

Only very young fresh, shelled beans are used in tagines; if the beans are more mature, peel them and the reduce cooking time. Dried broad beans are often used to make a bean soup or dip; they need to be first soaked for 48 hours in a cool place, changing the water 3–4 times, and the leathery skins removed before use. Dried, skinned broad beans are sold in North African and Middle Eastern food markets as skinned ful beans and will save time in preparation.

CAPSICUM (PEPPER)

Moroccans use a sweet pepper that is thinner-fleshed, not as broad as a capsicum, and tapering to a point. The *Capsicum* genus includes chillies.

CHARD

Also known as silverbeet and Swiss chard, it is a member of the beet family. The leaves are bright green and crinkly in texture, with a white rib running through the leaf widening into a stem.

CHICKPEAS

Skinned chickpeas are preferred as they absorb flavours better. Soak chickpeas overnight; the next day, lift up handfuls of chickpeas and rub them between your hands to loosen the skins, then skim the skins off as they float. Cover the chickpeas with fresh water and boil for at least 1 hour, until tender, or add to a stew or soup at the start of cooking. Tinned chickpeas may also be used, with skins removed in the same way. If preferred, leave skins on for all recipes as modern Moroccan cooks do. In terms of measurements, 220 g (8 oz/1 cup) dried chickpeas yields 2½ cups cooked, equivalent to 2 x 420 g (15 oz) tins.

CINNAMON

Finely shaved bark from the cinnamon tree, *Cinnamomum zeylanicum*, which is interleaved and rolled to form sticks or quills. Both sticks and ground cinnamon are widely used. Ground cinnamon often includes cassia, which is actually from another species of cinnamon tree. Cassia is more reddish-brown than cinnamon and can be used in place of cinnamon sticks; in fact, it is often sold as such. Cinnamon is used in savoury and sweet dishes and pastries.

CORIANDER (CILANTRO)

Essential in Moroccan cooking, fresh coriander has feathery green leaves with a rather pungent flavour. Coriander seeds are ground and used as a spice.

CORN ON THE COB

A popular street food, the sweet corn is cut from the plant, leaving a portion of the stem attached. Cobs are husked with the silk removed and then grilled over a charcoal fire. Before it is handed to the customer, the hot grilled cob is dipped into salted water, which makes it moist and very tasty, with a convenient handle already attached.

CORNMEAL, YELLOW

Dried yellow corn kernels ground to a meal are available in fine, medium and coarse grades from health food stores; choose the medium grade. Do not confuse with polenta, which is a granular form and not used in Morocco. Cornmeal is used to add to bread in rural areas, or for sprinkling on baking trays or on top of loaves to add crunch and flavour.

COUSCOUS

Made with coarse semolina grains and durum wheat flour. Semolina grains are sprinkled with lightly salted water and rolled with flour to form tiny pellets. This is still done by hand by some cooks, but these days machines are used. Both couscous purchased in bulk (regular couscous) and packets of instant couscous require steaming for the grains to swell properly and become light and fluffy. Regular couscous is found in Middle Eastern food stores; in supermarkets couscous is usually instant; if it is marked 'Maghrebi-style', it is regular couscous.

COUSCOUSSIER

The French name for the utensil in which couscous is steamed. The base is tall and slightly bulbous, with the steamer section fitted on top for cooking couscous. The traditional couscoussier of tin-lined copper does not have a lid, but the aluminium version usually does. The original couscoussier of the Berbers was earthenware.

CUMIN

With a warm, sweet aroma, yet pungent and earthy, cumin is one of the most popular spices in the region. Always select a darker cumin with a greenish-brown colour and oily texture. For the best flavour, use freshly ground seeds. A mixture of cumin and salt is a favourite condiment; for street food, it accompanies boiled eggs, pieces of mechoui (spit-roasted lamb), lamb kebabs and lamb liver kebabs. At the table, little bowls of the mixture are provided.

FIGS

This remarkable fruit has been important to the Mediterranean region from early days. The fresh fruit, both the purple (black) variety and the green, begins to appear early in summer. The majority of figs are consumed dried and are found in souk stalls strung on dried date-palm fronds like necklaces. The fresh fruit is enjoyed at the end of a meal, the dried for snacking and cooking.

FILO PASTRY

This thin pastry of the Eastern Mediterranean is not Moroccan, but it is the most easily available substitute outside Morocco for warkha pastry. Measurements have been given in the recipes regarding sheet sizes, which will serve as a guide for the size available in your area. However, most important is how it is handled. Thaw as directed on the package if frozen. Whether it is frozen or chilled, it must be left in its package at room temperature for 2 hours before use. Place the sheets flat on the work surface, and keep them covered with dry, folded cloths or plastic sheeting; never put damp cloths in contact with the pastry. Keep the kitchen cool and draught-free.

GINGER

Only dried ginger is used in Moroccan cooking, never fresh. Do not use more than is specified in recipes because too much ginger can impart a bitter taste.

HARISSA

A Tunisian condiment popular in Morocco, harissa is available from gourmet food stores and Middle Eastern markets, or make your own (see page 242). Use harissa with caution as it is extremely hot.

HONEY

Good Moroccan honeys are thick and aromatic with the flavour of herbs. If you can't find any Moroccan honey, use Mount Hymettus or other Greek thyme honey. Orange blossom honey is light and fragrant and is readily available.

MERGUEZ

A lamb sausage of Tunisian origin, which is popular in Morocco. It is spiced with harissa, paprika, allspice, fennel, black pepper, cumin and coriander seeds and flavoured with garlic. It is usually very hot, but the degree of heat depends on the manufacturer.

NIGELLA SEEDS

These little black seeds are usually sprinkled on bread before baking, and on steamed chicken. They have little aroma, but have a nutty flavour and are a little peppery. Black cumin seeds and black sesame seeds are often mistakenly called nigella seeds.

OLIVE OIL

Olive oil was, and is, used for salads, but there is an increasing trend in Morocco to replace smen in cooking with olive or other oils in the interests of better health. While specified throughout, as a general rule, extra virgin olive oil is recommended for salads, and the standard olive oil for cooking. Other vegetable oils are usually used for frying – sunflower oil, safflower oil and peanut oil.

ONION

The brown onion is used in most Moroccan cooking. Occasionally white onion is used; red onion is used in salads. Green onion is used as an accompaniment to some soups such as bissara in certain areas.

ORANGE FLOWER WATER

Also called orange blossom water, this is made from a distillation of the flowers of the bitter bigarade (seville) orange. It originated in the Middle East and was introduced to North Africa by the Arabs. Used to flavour beverages, and sweet and savoury food, it is also distilled in the home – see also 'rosewater'.

PAPRIKA

The paprika commonly used in Morocco is Spanish mild paprika. It is used as much for its colour as its flavour. Sweet Hungarian paprika may also be used.

PARSLEY

Flat-leaf (Italian) parsley is used. Alternatively, use curly parsley and include some stalks when chopping to increase its flavour in cooking.

POMEGRANATE

The Moroccans love colour, and the ruby red seeds of the pomegranate are scattered over fruit platters. Pomegranate juice is a favourite drink, and a citrus juicer is the best way to extract it, especially the type that has a hinged press attached. Removing the seeds is tedious as they must be separated from the pith (usually a few hard taps on the outside of a cut pomegranate held over a bowl can accomplish this). Fruit-juice extractors can graze the seeds, giving the juice a bitter flavour. Serve the chilled juice with a little rosewater. The pomegranate syrup sold in Middle Eastern stores is not used in Morocco.

PRESERVED LEMONS

Used in tagines and many Moroccan dishes to give a distinctive flavour. Make your own (see page 247) or buy those that are preserved in the

Moroccan manner (without oil) from gourmet food stores or good delicatessens.

PRUNES

The prune is the dried version of various species of the damascene (damson) plum. It is often a substitute for dates in meat and fruit tagines, but is increasingly used in its own right – an intensely flavoured sweet–sour fruit that marries well with spices. Today's prunes do not need soaking – they are moist and succulent and add a wonderful flavour to Moroccan dishes. While it is an easy (though sticky) task to remove the pits, pitted prunes are readily available.

QUINCE

A popular winter fruit used in tagines. While quince paste is not made in Morocco, it works well in recipes when quinces are not in season.

RAS EL HANOUT

A blend of many spices, which vary according to the maker. Some blends are kept a closely guarded secret. You can make your own version (see page 242) or buy a ready-made ground spice mix from gourmet food stores or specialist herb and spice stores.

RICE

Short- or medium-grained rice is preferred. It is used mainly in the north – Tangier, Tetuan and environs – where there is a stronger Spanish influence. However, Moroccans steam rice three times in a couscoussier, or in a colander lined with muslin (cheesecloth) over boiling water. Traditional rice-cooking methods have been used in the recipes.

ROSEWATER

A distillation of fragrant rose petals, originating in Persia and introduced to North Africa by the Arabs. In May, fresh rose petals and rosebuds are sold in souks. Many locals distil their own using an alembic, a superseded distiller that remains in use in Morocco and the Middle East. Where obtainable, orange blossoms (see 'orange flower

water') are also distilled. It is bottled and kept for 4–5 months before use and claimed to be superior to that made by distilleries. Rosewater is used to flavour beverages as well as sweet and savoury foods.

SAFFRON

The dried stigmas of *Crocus sativus*, regarded as the world's most expensive spice. Each flower consists of only three stigmas, which are hand-picked from the flowers, then dried. Introduced by the Arabs, saffron is grown, harvested and processed in Morocco. Threads and ground saffron are used as much for the beautiful yellow colour as for the aroma and flavour. Where a recipe calls for a pinch of ground saffron, use as much as sits on the very tip of a knife, as fingertips would take more than required. Only buy ground saffron from a reliable supplier.

SAFFRON, GROUND

Recipes in this book frequently call for ground saffron threads. To make your own ground saffron, the threads must be crisp. Put threads on a plate, place over boiling water and leave until dry and crisp. Transfer to a small mortar with a good pinch of salt. Using a pestle, pound to a powder.

SEMOLINA

Semolina is the milled inner endosperm of hard or durum wheat, pale beige or yellow in colour and granular in appearance. It can be very fine (almost like a flour), fine or coarse, the latter used in the manufacture of couscous. Fine and coarse semolina are sold as breakfast cereals. Very fine semolina is available at markets selling North African and Middle Eastern ingredients. Do not confuse semolina with semolina flour, which is used in pasta making, and is durum wheat flour.

SESAME SEEDS

Their use dating back some 4,000 years, sesame seeds have been part of the North African diet for millennia. It was the first seed from which oil was extracted for use in food, and while it isn't used in Morocco, the seeds certainly are. In fact, sesame seeds are a commercial crop. They are used to top Moroccan breads, toasted and sprinkled on savoury foods, toasted and ground to make ghoriba dial janjlane (page 196), and sprinkled on many sweet pastries. To toast the seeds, place seeds in a dry frying pan over medium heat. Stir often until lightly toasted, then tip immediately into a shallow dish to prevent them burning. When cool, store in a sealed jar in the refrigerator and use as required.

SHERIYA

Couscous is the 'pasta' of the Maghreb, however, there is a Moroccan pasta. Sheriya are pellets of dough rolled into thin strips a little thicker than vermicelli. They are usually steamed three times, and gently rubbed in cold water between steamings, then used in stuffings, or simply tossed with butter and served with sugar and cinnamon. However, most cooks these days prefer to crumble vermicelli to add to soups or to use in stuffings.

SMEN

A clarified (drawn) butter with milk solids that have been allowed to brown slightly, giving it a slightly nutty flavour (see page 243). Ghee can be used as a substitute; in many recipes, butter can also be used. An aged smen is made by the Berbers by storing the smen in an earthenware jar, which is then placed in the cellar or buried for a year or longer until it ages; it has a flavour resembling strong blue cheese.

TAGINE

An earthenware dish with a conical lid, and also the food cooked in this dish. Such food is really a stew or braise.

TANGIA

A pottery vessel shaped like a small amphora. The food cooked in it is also called tangia, known as the bachelor's dish; young men or soldiers away from home put chunks of meat (beef, lamb or goat) in it, add tomato, preserved lemon, sprigs of coriander (cilantro) and flat-leaf parsley, season and tie on parchment to cover it, making a handle with the string. This is taken to the hammam (bathhouse) furnace to be cooked on the embers for several hours.

YEAST

Active dried yeast is available in bulk or in 8 g (1/4 oz) sachets that each measure 2 teaspoons. Always store yeast in a sealed container in the refrigerator. For yeast past its use-by date, dissolve a teaspoon in 125 ml (4 fl oz/1/2 cup) warm water with 1 teaspoon sugar and leave it in a warm place for 15 minutes. If the yeast is frothy in this time, it can be used, otherwise discard it and purchase a fresh packet.

ZA'ATAR

The Arabic word for thyme. The Mediterranean climate gives certain wild herbs a pungency and flavour difficult to duplicate with cultivated herbs. If you cannot find dried za'atar from Morocco in food markets, use the dried thyme available at Greek markets or fresh lemon thyme; recipes indicate which substitutes are suitable. Do not confuse this with the Lebanese herb and spice mix of za'atar, used to sprinkle on bread.

INDEX

Published in 2008 by Murdoch Books, an imprint of Allen & Unwin

Murdoch Books Australia
83 Alexander Street
Crows Nest NSW 2065
Phone: +61 (0) 2 8425 0100
Fax: +61 (0) 2 9906 2218
www.murdochbooks.com.au
info@murdochbooks.com.au

Murdoch Books UK Limited
Erico House, 6th Floor
93–99 Upper Richmond Road
Putney, London SW15 2TG
Phone: +44 (0) 20 8785 5995
Fax: +44 (0) 20 8785 5985
www.murdochbooks.co.uk
info@murdochbooks.com.uk

Publisher: Lynn Lewis
Senior Designer: Heather Menzies
Series Design Concept: Sarah Odgers
Designer: Susanne Geppert
Project Manager: Justine Harding
Production: Alexandra Gonzalez
Text and recipes: Tess Mallos
Photographers: Alan Benson; Natasha Milne; Ashley Mackevicius,
Prue Ruscoe, Ian Hofstetter and Martin Brigdale
Index: Jo Rudd

National Library of Australia Cataloguing-in-Publication Data:
Title: Morocco.
ISBN: 9781741964394 (pbk.)
Series: World Kitchen.
Notes: Includes index.
Subjects: Cookery, Moroccan.
Dewey Number: 641.5961

A catalogue record for this book is available from the British Library.

Printed by 1010 Printing International Limited, China.
PRINTED IN CHINA. Reprinted 2010 (twice), 2011 (three times), 2013.